Bus Handbook

May 1996

British Bus Publishing

The North & West Wales Bus Handbook

The North & West Wales Bus Handbook is part of The Bus Handbook series that details the fleets of selective bus and coach operators. These Bus Handbooks are published by British Bus Publishing and cover Scotland, Wales and England north of London. The current list is shown at the end of the book. Together with similar books for southern England, published by Capital Transport which we also supply, they provide comprehensive coverage of all the principal operators' fleets in the British Isles. Handbooks for the FirstBus Group and Stagecoach are also published annually.

The operators included in this edition are those who are based in the former counties of Clwyd, Dyfed, Gwynedd and Powys. Also included are a number of those operators who provide significant coaching activities.

Quality photographs for inclusion in the series are welcome and a fee is payable. The publishers unfortunately cannot accept responsibility for any loss and request you show your name on each picture or slide. Details of changes to fleet information are also welcome.

To keep the fleet information up to date we recommend the Ian Allan publication, Buses published monthly, or for more detailed information, the PSV Circle monthly news sheets.

The writer and publisher would be glad to hear from readers should any information be available which corrects or enhances that given in this publication.

Series Editor: Bill Potter
Principal Editors for The North & West Wales Bus Handbook:
David Donati & John Jones

Acknowledgements:
We are grateful to Andy Chown, Tom Johnson, Vernon Morgan, The Crosville Enthusiasts' Club the PSV Circle and the operating companies for their assistance in the compilation of this book.

The cover photograph is by John Jones
Contents correct to May 1996

ISBN 1 897990 19 7
Published by British Bus Publishing Ltd
The Vyne, 16 St Margarets Drive, Wellington,
Telford, Shropshire, TF1 3PH
© British Bus Publishing, May 1996

CONTENTS

ACTON COACHES

D B Evans, 109 Herbert Jennings Avenue, Acton Park, Wrexham, LL12 7YA

Depot :Rhosddu Industrial Estate, Wrexham

LIB6352	Leyland Leopard PSU5C/4R	Duple Dominant II	C57F	1978	Ex Stephenson, Ryhope, 1988
XPP299X	Bedford YNT	Duple Dominant IV	C53F	1982	Ex Rover, Bromsgrove, 1990
607VYC	Volvo B10M-61	Plaxton Paramount 3500	C42FT	1983	Ex Provincial Tours, Manchester, 1994
TSV798	Van Hool T815H	Van Hool Alizée	C49FT	1984	Ex R&S Travel, Clifton, 1995
C483TAY	Ford Transit 190	Dormobile	B16F	1985	Ex Midland Fox, 1994
HIL3140	Bedford YNV Venturer	Duple 320	C57F	1986	Ex Swann, Blackpool, 1993
E180TWO	Freight Rover Sherpa	Carlyle Citybus 2	B20F	1988	Ex Cynon Valley, 1992

Previous Registrations:

607VYC	RME972Y		LIB6352	AAD185S		TSV798A	A163ERM
HIL3140	C200LGA, PR1787, C314XSC						

Livery: White and blue

During the early post-deregulation years, a large number of Carlyle-bodied Freight Rover Sherpas were built for National Welsh. Originally known as Bustlers they are now found in many parts of the country. An example of the Carlyle Citybus 2, E180TWO, was acquired by Acton Coaches from Cynon Valley. *John Jones*

ALPINE

Hughes Brothers (Llanrwst & Trefriw) Ltd, Builder Street West, Llandudno,
Conwy, LL30 1HH

Depots: Builder Street West, Llandudno; Central Coach Garage, Llanrwst; Marsh Road, Rhyl and Llanfairfechan.

CCC596	Guy Otter LL0D	Roe	FB25F	1954	Ex Preservation, 1993
HHG25	Leyland Tiger Cub PSUC1/1	East Lancashire	B43F	1959	Ex Burnley & Pendle, 1995
691DDE	Leyland Atlantean PDR1A/1	Northern Counties	O43/30D	1970	Ex Wall's, Sharston, 1993
JPL105K	Leyland Atlantean PDR1A/1	Park Royal	O43/24D	1972	Ex Crosville Cymru, 1995
NPD127L	Leyland National 1151/1R/0402		B49F	1973	Ex East Kent, 1988
XJA562L	Daimler Fleetline CRG6LXB	Northern Counties	H43/32F	1973	Ex Finglands, Manchester, 1994
GCY751N	Leyland National 11351/1R		B52F	1974	Ex Classic, Annfield Plain, 1995
LDC78P	Leyland Fleetline CRL6	Northern Counties	H43/31F	1975	Ex Camms, Nottingham, 1991
KBU912P	Leyland Atlantean AN68A/1R	Northern Counties	H43/32F	1975	Ex Finglands, Manchester, 1996
OFR117P	Leyland National 11351/2R		B52F	1976	Ex Halton, 1988
VUP850	Bedford YMT	Duple Dominant	C53F	1976	Ex Creams, Porthmadog, 1990
MDL651R	Bristol VRT/SL3/6LXB	Eastern Coach Works	H43/31F	1976	Ex Caelloi, Pwllheli, 1995
WMB298R	Bedford YMT	Plaxton Supreme III	C53F	1977	Ex George Edwards, Bwlchgwyn, 1994
PUF586R	Bristol VRT/SL3/6LXB	Eastern Coach Works	H43/31F	1977	Ex Caelloi, Pwllheli, 1995
WDM352R	Bristol VRT/SL3/501	Eastern Coach Works	H43/31F	1977	Ex Happy Days, Woodseaves, 1995
VCA181R	Leyland Fleetline FE30AGR	Northern Counties	H43/29F	1977	Ex Chester, 1990
VCA182R	Leyland Fleetline FE30AGR	Northern Counties	H43/29F	1977	Ex Chester, 1989
VCA183R	Leyland Fleetline FE30AGR	Northern Counties	H43/29F	1977	Ex Chester, 1989
BPT927S	Bristol VRT/SL3/6LXB	Eastern Coach Works	H43/31F	1977	Ex Northumbria, 1994
BPT928S	Bristol VRT/SL3/6LXB	Eastern Coach Works	H43/31F	1977	Ex Northumbria, 1994
TPE160S	Leyland National 11351A/1R(6HLXB)		B49F	1978	Ex Evag Cannon, Bolton, 1993
PJC630S	Ford R1114	Duple Dominant II	C53F	1978	Ex Creams, Porthmadog, 1990
CPT737S	Bristol VRT/SL3/6LXB	Eastern Coach Works	H43/31F	1978	Ex Northumbria, 1994
URF677S	Bristol VRT/SL3/501	Eastern Coach Works	H43/31F	1978	Ex PMT, 1994
FTU376T	Bristol VRT/SL3/501	Eastern Coach Works	H43/31F	1978	Ex Crosville Cymru, 1996
HUP768T	Bristol VRT/SL3/6LXB	Eastern Coach Works	H42/31F	1978	Ex Northumbria, 1994
TCC2T	Ford R1114	Duple Dominant II	C53F	1979	Ex Creams, Porthmadog, 1990
JAB7T	Bedford YMT	Van Hool Aragon	C53F	1979	Ex Royal Red, Llandudno, 1987
BRC838T	Bristol VRT/SL3/6LXB	Eastern Coach Works	H43/31F	1979	Ex Wall's, Northenden, 1995
BRC840T	Bristol VRT/SL3/6LXB	Eastern Coach Works	H43/31F	1979	Ex Wall's, Northenden, 1995
XSJ664T	Leyland Fleetline FE30AGR	Northern Counties	H44/31F	1979	Ex Green Buses, Bournemouth, 1995
VTD720T	Leyland Atlantean AN68A/1R	East Lancashire	O43/32F	1979	Ex Rossendale, 1994
SKF27T	Leyland National 11351A/1R (Volvo)		B49F	1979	Ex Tame Valley, Ashton, 1993
EUM893T	Leyland National 11351A/1R		B49F	1979	Ex Blue Bus, Horwich, 1992
OBR771T	Bristol VRT/SL3/6LXB	Eastern Coach Works	H43/31F	1979	Ex Tees & District, 1994
ECS884V	Leyland Fleetline FE30AGR	Northern Counties	H44/31F	1979	Ex Green Buses, Bournemouth, 1995
GRF712V	Bristol VRT/SL3/501	Eastern Coach Works	DPH39/28F	1980	Ex PMT, 1994
RMA442V	Bristol VRT/SL3/501	Eastern Coach Works	H43/31F	1980	Ex Crosville Cymru, 1996

Alpine operate a pair of Bedford YMT buses with Wadham Stringer bodywork that were new to Maidstone in 1982. The Vanguard design shown here has sold mostly for municipal and military application. Seen heading for Llandudno in all-red livery is TKM110X.

Alpine VCA181R is one of a trio of Northern Counties-bodied Leyland Fleetlines acquired from Chester in 1989-90, which are the longest serving double-decks in the fleet. It is seen near Rhos-on-Sea while waiting its turn at a Department of Transport roadside safety check. *John Jones*

BTX42V	Ford R1114	Plaxton Supreme IV	C53F	1980	Ex Owen, Llanrwst, 1981
HJB460W	Bristol VRT/SL3/6LXB	Eastern Coach Works	H43/31F	1980	Ex Wall's, Northenden, 1995
HJB463W	Bristol VRT/SL3/6LXB	Eastern Coach Works	H43/31F	1980	Ex Wall's, Northenden, 1995
TKM109X	Bedford YMT	Wadham Stringer Vanguard	B61F	1982	Ex Maidstone, 1987
TKM110X	Bedford YMT	Wadham Stringer Vanguard	B61F	1982	Ex Maidstone, 1987
GCC487Y	Ford R1114	Duple Dominant IV	C53F	1982	
OWD194	Aüwaerter Neoplan N122/3	Aüwaerter Skyliner	CH57/20CT	1982	Ex Yorkshire Voyager, 1992
951SAU	Aüwaerter Neoplan N122/3	Aüwaerter Skyliner	CH57/20CT	1984	Ex Yorkshire Voyager, 1992
A801LEY	Volvo B10M-61	Duple Laser	C57F	1984	
B567NCC	Bova EL28/581	Duple Calypso	C53F	1984	
B559KRY	Bova FHD12.280	Bova Futura	C49F	1985	Ex Starline, Wooton, 1995
B620OJC	Bedford YNT	Wright Contour	C53F	1985	
D257WEY	Bedford YNT	Duple 320	C53F	1987	
E661KCX	DAF SB2305DHS585	Duple 340	C57F	1988	Ex Redwing, Camberwell, 1993
E663KCX	DAF SB2305DHS585	Duple 340	C57F	1988	Ex Redwing, Camberwell, 1993
F42DJC	Iveco Daily 49.10	Robin Hood City Nippy	B25F	1989	
F43DJC	Iveco Daily 49.10	Robin Hood City Nippy	B25F	1989	
F916TTP	Mercedes-Benz 811D	Robin Hood	B25F	1990	
G142JCC	Iveco Daily 49.10	Phoenix	DP25F	1990	
G761HJC	Hestair Duple SDA1512	Duple 425	C57F	1990	
G762HJC	Hestair Duple SDA1512	Duple 425	C57F	1990	
M515ACC	Mercedes-Benz 709D	Marshall C19	B25F	1994	
N3ALP	Volvo B10M-62	Plaxton Première 320	C55F	1996	
N4ALP	Volvo B10M-62	Plaxton Première 320	C55F	1996	

Previous Registrations:

691DDE	STO534H	HHG25	HHG25, MBV402G	VUP850	KJC364P
951SAU	A103MWT	OWD194	BDV874Y	CCC596	From new

Livery: Red and white or white, red and orange (buses), white, red, orange, yellow and grey (coaches); green & cream (Guide Friday) JPL105K, VTD720T; green and white (Rhyl Bus & Coach Company)

Opposite top: **Representing the Alpine double-deck fleet is one of fifteen Bristol VRTs, GRF712V. Dating from 1980 when it was new to PMT, it is seen here in Llandudno.** *Paul Wigan*
Opposite bottom: **Leyland Nationals form the majority of the single-deck Alpine fleet, which includes SKF27T, new to Merseybus in 1979. Now powered by a Volvo engine, it is seen while operating a school contract at Llandrillo, near Rhos-on-sea.** *John Jones*

ARVONIA

R Morris, Arvonia Garage, The Square, Llanrug, Gwynedd, LL55 4AA

PSV412	Volvo B10M-61	Van Hool Alizee	C53F	1985	Ex Tellings - Golden Miller, 1987
C513TJF	Ford Transit 190	Alexander AM	B16F	1985	Ex Midland Fox, 1994
A2ARV	Volvo B10M-61	Caetano Algarve	C49FT	1986	Ex Coach Stop, Leigh-on-Sea, 1994
D158VRP	Mercedes-Benz L608D	Alexander AM	B20F	1986	Ex Alpine, Llandudno, 1995
F854YJX	DAF SB2305DHTD585	Duple 320	C49FT	1989	
367ARV	Volvo B10M-60	Van Hool Alizee	C49FT	1990	Ex Deeble, Darleyford, 1993
H521YCX	DAF SB2305DHS585	Duple 340	C57F	1991	Ex Blue Bus, Derby, 1995
J221HDS	Mercedes-Benz 811D	Carlyle	C19F	1992	Ex Patterson, Birmingham, 1995
L2ARV	Van Hool T815H	Van Hool Alicron	C49FT	1994	
M2ARV	EOS E180Z	EOS 90	C49FT	1995	
N ARV	EOS E180Z	EOS 90	C49FT	1996	

Previous Registrations:

A2ARV	C686KDS	PSV412	B998CUS, A2ARV	367ARV	G637CAF

Livery: White and red

Many Ford Transits that entered service even before deregulation day in October 1986 are still in use long after their original estimated service life of seven years. One of these reliable machines, C513TJF, is still giving a good account of itself with Arvonia though now eleven years old. *Paul Wigan*

BERWYN

B Japheth, Berwyn, Trefor, Gwynedd, LL54 5LY

WCD523K	Bristol VRT/SL2/6LX	Eastern Coach Works	H39/31F	1971	Ex Ellis Travel, Llangefni, 1995
GWD777T	Bedford YMT	Plaxton Supreme IV	C53F	1979	Ex George Edwards, Bwlchgwyn, 1993
SGR778V	Bristol VRT/SL3/6LXB	Eastern Coach Works	H43/31F	1979	Ex GHA Coaches, Bettws Gwerfil Goch, 1995
BCJ680V	Bedford YMT	Duple Dominant II	DP53F	1980	Ex Evans, Tregaron, 1994
MCH351W	Bedford YMT	Duple Dominant	B55F	1980	Ex George Edwards, Bwlchgwyn, 1995
KYU88X	Bedford YMQ	Wadham Stringer Vanguard	B41F	1982	Ex E Stott & Sons, Milnsbridge, 1995
JST905Y	Mercedes-Benz L508D	Reeve Burgess	C19F	1982	Ex Martin, Fort Augustus, 1986
A343ASF	Mercedes-Benz L608D	Stevensons	B16FL	1983	Ex Stevensons, 1994
B44MRF	Bedford YMP	Plaxton Paramount 3200	C35F	1984	Ex Byses Sarn, 1992
A5NPT	Leyland Tiger TRCTL11/3R	Duple Laser	C51FT	1986	Ex Evans, Tregaron, 1996
D219GLJ	Freight Rover Sherpa	Dormobile	B16F	1987	Ex North Western, 1991
D564HNW	Iveco Daily 49.10	Robin Hood City Nippy	DP21F	1986	Ex Evans, Tregaron, 1995
AAZ9102	Mercedes-Benz 609D	Reeve Burgess Beaver	C23F	1988	Ex Dodsworth, Boroughbridge, 1994
H544KSG	Iveco Daily 49.10	Carlyle Dailybus 2	B25F	1990	Ex William Hamilton, Maybole, 1994
J248SOC	Iveco Daily 49.10	Carlyle Dailybus 2	B25F	1991	Ex Llynfi Coaches, 1993

Previous Registrations:

A5NPT	C242HBH	AAZ9102	E91NVH

Livery: White, yellow and brown

Several operators have begun commercial operations in the Caernarfon area in recent years, joining some of the well known firms which have been around for many years. A343ASF, a Mercedes-Benz L608D with a PSV conversion by Stevensons is owned by Berwyn, an operator based at Trefor, mid-way between Caernarfon and Pwllheli. Berwyn's main route connects the two towns. *Paul Wigan*

Browns of Builth E737EVJ is pictured in The Square, Brecon. Currently around a dozen Powys services are time-tables for Browns mostly one-day-per-week from Builth to, inter alia, Llanwrtyd Wells, Kington and Aberedw. A Rhayader to Hereford service and the staple Llandrindod Wells to Brecon require a more substantial involvement. New purchases for rural operators have to earn their keep on a variety of work. As such, L710LFO, a mark III Caetano Optimo-bodied Toyota, can be seen on schedule service in addition to private hire. Here, however, the vehicle was in Sofia Gardens, Cardiff on the occasion of a rugby international. *John Jones*

BROWNS of BUILTH

DJ & NW Brown, 15 High Street, Builth Wells, Powys, LD1 5RY.

Depot :Tynrheol, Hundred House

RCJ211M	Bedford VAS5	Plaxton Panorama IV	C29F	1974	Ex Bengry, Leominster, 1986
PBH539R	Bedford YMT	Plaxton Supreme III	C53F	1977	Ex Grange, East Ham, 1989
EGR704S	Bedford VAS5	Plaxton Supreme III	C29F	1978	Ex Grimstead, Patchway, 1992
FYA201T	Bedford YLQ	Duple Dominant II Express	C45F	1979	Ex Coombs, Weston-super-Mare, 1995
CFO700V	Bedford YMT	Duple Dominant II	C53F	1980	Ex Canyon, Hereford, 1984
DBX555W	Bedford YLQ	Duple Dominant II Express	C45F	1980	Ex Coombs, Weston-super-Mare, 1995
EAA829W	Bedford YMQ	Duple Dominant II	C45F	1980	Ex Coombs, Weston-super-Mare, 1995
JVJ511Y	Bedford YNT	Duple Dominant IV	C53F	1982	Ex Central Coachways, 1992
A511LPP	Bedford YMP	Plaxton Paramount 3200	C35F	1983	Ex Whites Coaches, Berinsfield, 1992
A945MDH	Bedford YNT	Plaxton Paramount 3200	C49F	1984	Ex Central Coachways, 1992
A946MDH	Bedford YNT	Plaxton Paramount 3200	C49F	1984	Ex Central Coachways, 1992
A373XTG	Bedford CF	Dormobile	M12	1984	Ex private owner, 1994
B804TCJ	Bedford CF	Dormobile	M12	1984	Ex Humphreys, Llanfaredd, 1988
B955BSU	Bedford CFL	Scott	M12	1985	Ex Porteous, Wigan, 1995
C410WCJ	Bedford CF	Dormobile	M12	1985	
C167XFO	Bedford CF	Dormobile	M12	1986	
D110CRE	Freight Rover Sherpa	PMT	DP16F	1986	Ex PMT, 1993
D914BFO	Bedford CF	Steedrive Parflo	M12	1987	Ex Sargeants, Llanfaredd, 1988
D915BFO	Bedford CF	Dormobile	M12	1987	Ex Sargeants, Llanfaredd, 1988
D416BCJ	Bedford CFL	Steedrive Parflo	M12	1987	
D614GDU	Bedford YNT	Plaxton Paramount 3200 III	C53F	1987	Ex Vanguard, Bedworth, 1990
E737EVJ	Bedford YMP	Plaxton Paramount 3200 III	C35F	1987	
E76PUH	Freight Rover Sherpa	Carlyle Citybus 2	B20F	1987	Ex Cynon Valley, 1992
E329EVH	DAF MB230LT615	Plaxton Paramount 3500 III	C53F	1988	Ex Smiths, Alcester, 1989
E147TBO	MCW MetroRider MF150/78	MCW	B23F	1988	Ex Cardiff Bus, 1996
E148TBO	MCW MetroRider MF150/79	MCW	DP23F	1988	Ex Cardiff Bus, 1996
E149TBO	MCW MetroRider MF150/79	MCW	DP23F	1988	Ex Cardiff Bus, 1996
G767RVJ	Freight Rover Sherpa	Crystals	C16F	1989	
G799RNC	Leyland Tiger TRCTL11/3RZ	Duple 320	C53F	1989	Ex Shearings, 1994
H399CJF	DAF SB2305DHS585	Caetano Algarve	C53F	1990	Ex Brittain's, Northampton, 1993
L710LFO	Toyota Coaster HZB50R	Caetano Optimo III	C21F	1994	

Previous Registrations:
D614GDU   D677FWK, 4828VC

Livery: White and maroon

Browns of Builth operate two DAF SB230s the newer carries the Caetano Algarve body, a later version of the Algarve 88 model. The livery is white with maroon banding.
John Jones

Bryn Melyn is unusual in 1996 that, aside from three Mercedes-Benz minibuses, the five coaches operated are all Ford R1114s, all with Plaxton Supreme bodywork. Typical of these is XGR445V, seen after a rain shower at Cefn Mawr. *John Jones*

J38VDW is one of a pair of Carlyle-bodied Iveco Daily minibuses new to Bebbs now in the Caelloi fleet. One was regularly to be found on the Pwllheli to Porthmadog service though a new Dennis Dart with Plaxton Pointer body has taken over this duty. J38VDW is seen in the attractive main street in Porthmadog. *John Jones*

BRYN MELYN

Bryn Melyn Motor Services Ltd, Abbey Road Garage, Llangollen,
Denbighshire, LL20 8SN

CBM293T	Ford R1114	Plaxton Supreme IV	C53F	1978	Ex Blueways, Battersea, 1992
BNT667T	Ford R1114	Plaxton Supreme IV	C53F	1979	Ex Britannia, Telford, 1992
JFK866V	Ford R1114	Plaxton Supreme IV Express	C53F	1979	Ex Britannia, Telford, 1991
XGR445V	Ford R1114	Plaxton Supreme IV	C53F	1980	Ex Pearce, Yatton, 1992
GNT435V	Ford R1114	Plaxton Supreme IV	C53F	1980	Ex Britannia, Telford, 1994
J544DJC	Mercedes-Benz 814D	Autobus Classique	C33F	1992	
J912PEY	Mercedes-Benz 410D	North West Coach Sales	M15	1992	
L495XNR	Mercedes-Benz 814D	Dormobile Routemaker	DP33F	1993	

Livery: White, blue, yellow and red

CAELLOI

T H, E, EB & N Jones, West End Garage, Pwllheli, Gwynedd, LL53 5PH

FOD941Y	Bedford YMT	Plaxton Bustler	B55F	1983	Ex Rider York, 1993
E910UNW	Volvo B10M-61	Plaxton Paramount 3500 III	C48FT	1988	Ex Wallace Arnold, 1992
F977DEY	Volvo B10M-61	Plaxton Paramount 3500 III	C49FT	1989	
F317VVC	Volvo B10M-60	Plaxton Paramount 3500 III	C44FT	1989	Ex Harry Shaw, Coventry, 1990
G500LWU	Volvo B10M-60	Plaxton Paramount 3500 III	C48FT	1990	Ex Wallace Arnold, 1993
J37VDW	Iveco Daily 49.10	Carlyle Dailybus 2	B25F	1992	Ex Cousins Coaches, Belmont, 1995
J38VDW	Iveco Daily 49.10	Carlyle Dailybus 2	B25F	1992	Ex Cousins Coaches, Belmont, 1995
L10CAE	Volvo B10M-60	Plaxton Excalibur	C49FT	1994	
M378BJC	Volvo B10M-62	Plaxton Premiére 350	C49FT	1995	
N418EJC	Volvo B10M-62	Plaxton Premiére 350	C49FT	1996	
N459EEY	Dennis Dart 9.8SDL30..	Plaxton Pointer	B40F	1996	

Livery: White, red orange and yellow.

Previous Registrations:
F317VVC   F804UDU, KOV2

CARREGLEFN COACHES

A W Lewis, Carreglefn Garage, Carreglefn, Anglesey LL68 OPR

GCC572	Commer Avenger TS3	Duple Corinthian	C41F	1959	Ex preservation, 1995
MVC12P	Bedford YRT	Plaxton Supreme III Express	C53F	1976	Ex Fallon, Dunbar, 1982
KJC97	Volvo B58-56	Duple Dominant	C53F	1976	Ex Caelloi, Pwllheli, 1986
AKK172T	Bedford YMT	Duple Dominant	B61F	1978	Ex Berwyn Coaches, 1992
GEY371	Volvo B10M-61	Duple Dominant	C51F	1982	Ex Evans, Tregaron, 1994
997EAY	Volvo B10M-61	Plaxton Viewmaster IV	C51F	1981	Ex Caelloi, Pwllheli, 1990
GEY124	Volvo B10M-61	Plaxton Paramount 3500	C53F	1984	Ex Griffiths, Port Dinorwig, 1993
NJC393	Volvo B10M-61	Plaxton Paramount 3200 II	C53F	1986	Ex Brittain's, Northampton, 1991
D613WEY	Freight Rover Sherpa	Dormobile	B16F	1986	Ex Bee Line Buzz, 1990
D722JUB	Freight Rover Sherpa	Carlyle	B16F	1986	Ex Oare's of Holywell, 1992
H547EVM	Ford Transit VE6	Made-to-Measure	C20F	1991	Ex Browns, Bathgate, 1995

Previous Registrations:

997EAY	JSJ434W	GEY124	A279GFF	KJC97	NHP225P
D613WEY	D738PTU, GEY124	GEY371	WUD322X	NJC393	C124PNH

Livery: Blue and cream/white

CELTIC TRAVEL

JP & GM Jones, New Street, Llanidloes, Powys SY18 6EH

NPU983M	Bristol VRT/SL3/6LX	Eastern Coach Works	H39/31F	1973	Ex Eastern National, 1989
NVJ603R	Bedford YLQ	Plaxton Supreme III Express	C45F	1976	Ex Williams, Brecon, 1992
XWX161S	Leyland Leopard PSU5C/4R	Duple Dominant II	C57F	1978	Ex Baker, Enstone, 1994
ATV182T	Bedford YMT	Willowbrook	B55F	1978	Ex Beeline, Warminster, 1991
BBB544V	Bedford YMT	Plaxton Supreme IV	C53F	1980	Ex Moor-Dale, Newcastle, 1982
KYC984V	Volvo B58-56	Plaxton Supreme IV	C53F	1980	Ex Roman City, Bath, 1984
FCY296W	Bedford YMQ	Duple Dominant	B45F	1981	Ex Martin Perry, Bromyard, 1992
FCY297W	Bedford YMQ	Duple Dominant	B45F	1981	Ex County, 1993
349LVO	Volvo B10M-61	Jonckheere Jubilee P50	C51FT	1983	Ex Tellings, Byfleet, 1987
A606UGD	Volvo B10M-61	Van Hool Alizée	C49FT	1984	Ex Park's, 1988
C486TPG	Mercedes-Benz L608D	Coachcraft	C27F	1986	Ex Stanley Gath, Dewsbury, 1988
H759RNT	Van Hool T815	Van Hool Alizée	C49FT	1991	Ex Williamsons, Shrewsbury, 1993

Previous Registrations:

349LVO	ONV652Y

Livery: Cream and green (coaches); silver & grey (executive coaches); red and cream (buses)

Situated in North Anglesey, near the village of Carreglefn, is the Carreglefn coaches base. This fleet contains just one full-size bus, AKK172T, a Duple Dominant-bodied Bedford YMT and part of a batch of six delivered to Maidstone Borough Council in 1978. The 3+2 seating arrangement allows 61 seated passengers. *Paul Wigan*

Now 23 years old, NPU983M still performs useful work in the Celtic Travel fleet. Several members of the same batch of these former Eastern National vehicles have given good service to operators in mid and north Wales including NPU981M with Padarn and NPU982M still with Express Motors. *John Jones*

Former Warrington Transport vehicles have seldom featured in the fleet of a Welsh operator. There is one presently, NED352M, a Daimler Fleetline bodied by East Lancashire. Acquired in 1992 by Cerbydau Cenarth Coaches, it is seen operating a school contract at Llandysul in March 1996. *John Jones*

The current Cerbydau Cenarth Coaches fleet of thirteen vehicles contains no less than nine chassis marques. A relatively unusual vehicle is TJI5843, a Jonckheere Jubilee-bodied Mercedes-Benz 0303 originally registered A126SNH. This attractive vehicle is seen at Aberaeron. *John Jones*

CERBYDAU CENARTH COACHES

WG James and DCR & AWL James, Falls Garage, Cenarth, Newcastle Emlyn, Cardiganshire SA38 9JP

NED352M	Daimler Fleetline CRG6LX	East Lancashire	H43/29F	1973	Ex Warrington, 1992
NWO731	DAF MB200DKL600	Plaxton Supreme IV	C55F	1978	Ex Wealden, Five Oak Green, 1992
WWL532T	AEC Reliance 6U2R	Duple Dominant II Express	C49F	1979	Ex Heyfordian, Upper Heyford, 1994
DAD254T	Leyland Leopard PSU5C/4R	Plaxton Supreme IV	C57F	1979	Ex Silcox, Pembroke Dock, 1990
JTV465V	Bedford CFL	Reeve Burgess Reebur	C17F	1980	Ex Pedder, Enfield, 1993
GWE502V	Ford R1114	Duple Dominant II	C53F	1980	Ex Walker, Walsall, 1988
MNM26V	Bedford YLQ	Plaxton Supreme IV	C33F	1980	Ex Walker, New Greencroft, 1990
SND297X	Leyland Leopard PSU5C/4R	Plaxton Supreme V	C49FT	1981	Ex Wilkins, Cymmer, 1989
FNE516Y	Mercedes-Benz L508D	Dixon Lomas	C21F	1983	Ex Athelstan, Chippenham, 1990
TJI5843	Mercedes-Benz 0303	Jonckheere Jubilee P50	C49FT	1984	Ex Executive Travel, Wednesfield, 1995
LBZ7534	Volkswagen LT55	Optare City Pacer	C21F	1987	Ex Heslop, Whitehaven, 1995
F747SBX	Renault Master T35D	Coachwork Walker	M16	1988	
G869YBX	Renault Trafic	Holdsworth	M14	1989	

Previous Registrations:

LBZ7534	D555TMR	NWO731	YDG500S	WWL532T	YPL103T, 9945NE
TJI5843	A126SNH, 203YKX, 3655RE, A17ETS				

Livery: White, red, orange and yellow

The number of AEC Reliances is steadily declining though many of this once-popular marque are to be found listed in this book. One is Cerbydun Cenarth Coaches WWL532T which, when new as YPL103T, formed part of a large fleet bodied by Duple and Plaxton acquired to modernise the Green Line operation of London Country. *John Jones*

CLWYDIAN TOURS

RD & ML Evans and LA Rawson, Station Road Garage, Pentre Llanrhaeadr,
Denbighshire LL16 4NT

BUX204L	Bedford YRQ	Duple Dominant	C45F	1973	Ex Whittle, Highley, 1975
OBO666M	Bedford YRT	Duple Dominant Express	C53F	1974	Ex Davies, Pen-y-graig, 1977
UUX841S	Bedford YMT	Plaxton Supreme III Express	C53F	1978	Ex Vagg, Knockin Heath, 1983
ACA912S	Bedford YMT	Duple Dominant	C53F	1978	
YRY508T	Bedford YLQ	Plaxton Supreme III	C45F	1978	Ex Lester's, Long Whatton, 1979
846MBF	Bedford YMT	Plaxton Supreme IV	C53F	1979	
9284UN	Bedford YNT	Duple Dominant IV	C53F	1982	Ex Johnson, Hanslope, 1990
ODM101	Volvo B10M-61	Duple Dominant IV	C57F	1982	
MSV372	Ford R1114	Duple Dominant IV	C53F	1983	
B40BCA	Ford Transit 160	Deansgate	M12	1984	
C543HCA	Ford R1115	Plaxton Paramount 3200 II	C53F	1985	
D700STU	Leyland Tiger TRCTL11/3RZ	Plaxton Paramount 3200 II	C57F	1987	
F130DMB	Iveco Daily 49.10	Wright	C25F	1988	
F721KCA	Dennis Javelin 11SDA1906	Duple 320	C57F	1989	
G144RCA	Dennis Javelin 12SDA1907	Duple 320	C57F	1990	
H712BRG	Toyota Coaster HDB30R	Caetano Optimo II	C21F	1990	Ex Garnett, Tindale Crescent, 1992
M829VCA	Dennis Javelin 12SDA2136	Caetano Algarve II	C57F	1994	

Previous Registrations:

846MBF	JMA880T	MSV372	NCA520Y
9284UN	XPP283X	ODM101	KCA181Y

Livery: White and blue; Peter Evans & Son fleetname is also used.

CHALONER'S

EJ & E Chaloner, Pendwll Road, Moss, Wrexham LL11 6EU

H738TWB	Mercedes-Benz 811D	Reeve Burgess Beaver B33F	1990

Livery: White and blue

Chaloner's single vehicle is this Mercedes-Benz 811 with Reeve Burgess Beaver bodywork new in 1990. It is seen at Moss Well, a location only serviced by the first journey to, and the last and 12:15 departures from Wrexham bus station. The picturesque nature of Moss Valley can be seen through the downpour.
Tom Johnson

It is almost twenty years since OBO666M was acquired by Clwydian Tours from the old established Sidney Davies, Pen-y-Graig fleet. Despite it's age, this Duple Dominant bodied Bedford YRT has been maintained in immaculate condition as shown in this view taken at Rhos-on-sea. *John Jones*

Although the majority of the Clwydian Tours fleet are Bedfords, a couple of Fords and a Leyland Tiger are used, latterly joined by three Dennis Javelins. The full size fleet is completed by ODM101, a Volvo B10M which carries one of the last Duple Dominant bodies built. *John Jones*

CLYNNOG & TREFOR

Clynnog & Trefor Motor Co Ltd, The Garage, Trefor, Gwynedd, LL54 5HP.

MTV503P	Bedford YMT	Plaxton Supreme III Express	DP53F	1976	Ex Barton, Chilwell, 1984
PEH654R	Bristol VRT/SL3/501	Eastern Coach Works	H43/31F	1976	Ex Roberts, Maerdy, 1992
SNN159R	Bristol VRT/SL3/6LXB	Eastern Coach Works	H43/31F	1977	Ex Southend, 1992
STL199R	Bedford YMT	Plaxton Supreme III Express	C53F	1977	Ex Nefyn Coaches, 1985
TRM15S	Ford R1114	Plaxton Supreme III	C53F	1977	Ex Byses Sarn, 1983
YBF678S	Bristol VRT/SL3/501	Eastern Coach Works	H43/31F	1978	Ex Roberts, Maerdy, 1992
JMB404T	Bristol VRT/SL3/501	Eastern Coach Works	H43/31F	1979	Ex Primrose Coaches, Hayle, 1994
BTO291T	Bedford VAS5	Plaxton Supreme III	C29F	1978	Ex Hardy, Crook, 1994
BFJ209T	Bedford YMT	Plaxton Supreme IV	C53F	1979	Ex Evans, Tregaron, 1996
USU192	Volvo B58-56	Plaxton Supreme IV	C53F	1979	Ex Godson, Crossgates, 1995
GRF697V	Bristol VRT/SL3/501	Eastern Coach Works	H43/31F	1979	Ex PMT, 1992
CCP433V	Ford R1114	Duple Dominant II	C53F	1980	Ex Stubbs, Manchester, 1984
34BCG	Volvo B58-56	Plaxton Supreme IV	C53F	1980	Ex Tappins, Didcot, 1994
XSU653	Volvo B10M-61	Duple Goldliner IV	C49FT	1982	Ex Taw & Torridge, Merton, 1995
PJI6067	Volvo B10M-61	Duple Goldliner IV	C51F	1982	Ex Fletcher, Offerton, 1995
EJC412X	Volvo B10M-61	Duple Goldliner IV	C51F	1982	Ex Evans, Tregaron, 1996
ESU294	Bedford YMT	Plaxton Supreme V Express	C53F	1982	Ex Clarkes of London, 1986
D128NON	Freight Rover Sherpa	Carlyle	B18F	1987	Ex J C, Widnes, 1993
D142NON	Freight Rover Sherpa	Carlyle	B18F	1987	Ex McKleans, Whitney, 1996
D109WCC	Freight Rover Sherpa	Carlyle	B18F	1987	Ex Woods, Falkirk, 1994
D114WCC	Freight Rover Sherpa	Carlyle	B18F	1987	Ex Woods, Fallark, 1994
SSU632	Volvo B10M-61	Jonckheere Jubilee P599	C53FT	1988	Ex KMP, Llanberis, 1995
HSU548	Volvo B10M-61	Jonckheere Jubilee P599	C53FT	1988	Ex KMP, Llanberis, 1996
YSU446	Volvo B10M-60	Plaxton Paramount 3500 III	C48FT	1989	Ex Wallace Arnold, 1993
FSU106	Volvo B10M-60	Plaxton Paramount 3500 III	C50F	1990	Ex Wallace Arnold, 1994

Previous Registrations:

34BCG	DJB866V	PJI6067	FHS759X
EJC412X	FHS751X, OJC496	SSU632	E77AEY, 7CCH, E246AJC
ESU294	BGS299X	USU192	OVH624T
FSU106	G516LWU	XSU653	FHS745X, NDO856, YFJ759X
HSU548	E773YJC, A7KMP, E264AJC	YSU446	F403DUG

Livery: Cream, red and orange

The Clynnog & Trefor double deck fleet has been reduced to five since the last edition of this Handbook following the sale of the former London Buses DMS. Those remaining are all Eastern Coach Works-bodied Bristol VRTs represented here by YBF678S seen about to turn off the A499 to serve its home village of Trefor while operating the Caernarfon to Pwllheli service. *John Jones*

CROSS GATES COACHES

Cross Gates Coaches Ltd, Cross Gates, Llandrindod Wells, Powys   LD1 6RE

NJV217R	AEC Reliance 6U3ZR	Plaxton Supreme III	C53F	1977	Ex Evans, Tregaron, 1993
RVU539R	AEC Reliance 6U3ZR	Plaxton Supreme III	C53F	1977	Ex Williams, Brecon, 1992
WAX186S	AEC Reliance 6U3ZR	Plaxton Supreme III	C46FT	1978	Ex Evans, Tregaron, 1993
BEC819S	Bedford YLQ	Duple Dominant II	C45F	1978	Ex Evans, Tregaron, 1993
CUT402T	AEC Reliance 6U3ZR	Plaxton Supreme IV	C53F	1979	Ex Gretton, Peterborough, 1993
APH523T	DAF MB200DKL600	Plaxton Supreme IV	C57F	1979	Ex Harrow Contract Services, 1994
PPT910	Mercedes-Benz 0303	Plaxton Supreme IV	C49F	1980	Ex Williams, Brecon, 1995
7074DK	Leyland Tiger TRCTL11/2R	Plaxton Supreme VI Express	C53F	1982	Ex Hills of Tredegar, 1991
A178SHD	Quest VM	Plaxton Paramount 3200	C53F	1984	Ex Stott, New Mill, 1993
529FN	Scania K112CRS	Van Hool Alizée	C49FT	1984	Ex British Airways, 1985
RYX492	Scania K112CRS	Van Hool Alizée	C49FT	1984	Ex Hills Services, Stibb Cross, 1990
HIL7896	Leyland Royal Tiger RT	Van Hool Alizée	C49FT	1986	Ex Pullman, Crofty, 1994
H825RWJ	Scania K113CRB	Van Hool Alizée	C55F	1991	Ex Boon's, Boreham, 1995
N591WND	Mercedes-Benz 709D	Alexander Sprint	B27F	1996	
N10CGC	Scania K113CRB	Irizar Century 12.35	C49FT	1996	

Previous Registrations:

529FN	B187VPP	PPT910	NMJ297V, 8914RU
7074DK	NDW142X	RYX492	B188VPP
A178SHD	A821LEL, 319BHR, A290MSH, A14ESS		
HIL7896	C520UNP	WAX186S	YRY935S, PPT910

Livery: Turquoise and white

Powys County Council have recast the network of infrequent services that link the towns of Llandrindod Wells, Builth Wells, Rhayader and Newbridge-on-Wye. The result is a more intensive service that better utilises resources. To operate it, Cross Gates have leased this Alexander Sprint-bodied Mercedes-Benz as an experiment for a year. Loadings will judge the future of this initiative. N591WND is seen in Builth Wells. *David Donati*

CROSVILLE CYMRU

Crosville Wales Ltd, Imperial Buildings, Glan-y-Mor Road, Llandudno Junction LL31 9RH

A subsidiary of British Bus plc.
Depot and outstations: Aberystwyth; Amlwch; Bangor; Caego; Caernarfon; Corwen; Denbigh; Dolgellau; Holyhead; Holywell; Llandudno Junction; Llanrhystyd; Llanrwst; Machynlleth; Mold; New Quay; Pwllheli; Rhyl and Tregaron.

Single deck vehicles:

SLC27	K27EWC	Leyland Lynx LX2R11C15Z4R	Leyland Lynx 2	B49F	1992	Ex Colchester, 1994
SLG28	H28MJN	Leyland Lynx LX2R11G15Z4R	Leyland Lynx	B49F	1991	Ex Colchester, 1994
SLG29	H29MJN	Leyland Lynx LX2R11G15Z4R	Leyland Lynx	B49F	1991	Ex Colchester, 1994
SLC30	H130LPU	Leyland Lynx LX2R11C15Z4R	Leyland Lynx	B49F	1990	Ex Colchester, 1994
SLL31	D31RWC	Leyland Lynx LX112TL11FR1	Leyland Lynx	B49F	1986	Ex Colchester, 1994
SLL32	D32RWC	Leyland Lynx LX112TL11FR1	Leyland Lynx	B49F	1986	Ex Colchester, 1994

SLC33-37		Leyland Lynx LX112L10ZR1	Leyland Lynx	B49F	1988-89	Ex Colchester, 1994

33	E33EVW	34	E34EVW	35	E35EVW	36	E36EVW	37	E37EVW

SLC38	G38YHJ	Leyland Lynx LX2R11C15Z4R	Leyland Lynx	B49F	1989	Ex Colchester, 1994
SLC39	G39YHJ	Leyland Lynx LX2R11C15Z4R	Leyland Lynx	B49F	1989	Ex Colchester, 1994
SLC40	G40YHJ	Leyland Lynx LX2R11C15Z4R	Leyland Lynx	B49F	1989	Ex Colchester, 1994
CTL48	C248SPC	Leyland Tiger TRCTL11/3RH	Duple 320	C53F	1986	Ex Luton & District, 1995
CTL63	C63JTU	Leyland Tiger TRCTL11/3RH	Duple 340	C49FT	1986	Ex Crosville 1986

SLC66-70		Leyland Lynx LX112L10ZR1R	Leyland Lynx	B49F	1989	Ex Chesterfield, 1995

66	F66FKW	67	F67FKW	68	F68FKW	69	F69FKW	70	F70FKW

Opposite top: **Aberystwyth is the midway point on the joint Crosville Cymru/Rhondda 701 route that links Holyhead and Cardiff. Having worked the northern section, CTL48, C248SPC is seen awaiting the arrival of the Rhondda coach from Cardiff before returning north.** *John Jones*
Opposite bottom: **Leyland Lynx SLC66, F66FKW from Chesterfield.** *John Jones*
Below: **Following a brief flirtation with Leyland National Greenways, all of which have now left, Crosville Cymru received twenty-three Leyland Lynx, making them the most numerous single-deck type in the fleet. SLG299, E299OMG is one of two acquired from Atlas Bus in 1994 and is seen entering the bus station at Rhyl.** *John Jones*

Crosville Cymru retain a small number of coaches for use primarily on longer services. Most are Leyland Tigers, that, in 1994, were joined by a pair of Volvo B10Ms from Moor-Dale. CVV593, HIL7593, which has a Duple 340 body, was registered E180FFT when new. The vehicle is seen at Caernarfon.
Paul Wigan

CTL81	FAZ5181	Leyland Tiger TRCTL11/3R	Plaxton Paramount 3200 E	C51F	1984	Ex Luton & District, 1995
CTL83	SIB8583	Leyland Tiger TRCTL11/3R	Plaxton Paramount 3200 E	C51F	1984	Ex Luton & District, 1994
CTL89	SIB7689	Leyland Tiger TRCTL11/3RH	Duple 320	C53F	1986	Ex Luton & District, 1994
CTL92	SIB9492	Leyland Tiger TRCTL11/3R	Plaxton Paramount 3200 E	C53F	1984	Ex Luton & District, 1994
CTL93w	FAZ3193	Leyland Tiger TRCTL11/3RH	Duple 320	C53F	1986	Ex Luton & District, 1995
CTL94	FAZ3194	Leyland Tiger TRCTL11/3RH	Duple 320	C53F	1986	Ex Luton & District, 1995
SLG299	E299OMG	Leyland Lynx LX112TL11ZR1S	Leyland Lynx	B49F	1988	Ex Atlas Bus, 1994
SLC328	E328OMG	Leyland Lynx LX112TL11ZR1S	Leyland Lynx	B49F	1988	Ex Atlas Bus, 1994
SNL365	VKE563S	Leyland National 11351A/1R		B49F	1977	Ex Maidstone & District, 1995
SNL386	YPL386T	Leyland National 10351B/1R		B41F	1978	Ex London & Country, 1994
SNL387	YPL387T	Leyland National 10351B/1R		B41F	1978	Ex London & Country, 1994
SNL443	YPL443T	Leyland National 10351B/1R		B41F	1978	Ex London & Country, 1994
SMM501	M501AJC	MAN 11.190	Optare Vecta	B43F	1995	
SMM502	M502AJC	MAN 11.190	Optare Vecta	B43F	1995	
SMM503	M503AJC	MAN 11.190	Optare Vecta	B43F	1995	
SMM504	M504AJC	MAN 11.190	Optare Vecta	B43F	1995	

SNL558-673

		Leyland National 10351B/1R		B44F	1978-79 Ex Crosville, 1986		

558	HMA558T	572	JTU572T	576	JTU576T	600	JTU600T	664	GMB664T
563	HMA563T	573	JTU573T	589	JTU589T	648	GMB648T	673	MCA673T
571	HMA571T	574	JTU574T	590	JTU590T	660	GMB660T		

CVV592	HIL7592	Volvo B10M-61	Duple 340	C51FT	1988	Ex Moor-Dale, 1994
CVV593	HIL7593	Volvo B10M-61	Duple 340	C51FT	1988	Ex Moor-Dale, 1994
SDD701	F701ECC	DAF SB220LC550	Optare Delta	DP48F	1989	
SDD702	F702ECC	DAF SB220LC550	Optare Delta	DP48F	1989	
SLC967	E967PME	Leyland Lynx LX112TL11ZR1R(L10)	Leyland Lynx	B49F	1988	Ex Atlas Bus, 1994
SLC968	E968PME	Leyland Lynx LX112TL11ZR1R(L10)	Leyland Lynx	B49F	1988	Ex Atlas Bus, 1994

Route branding was re-introduced by Crosville Cymru in April 1996 following the cessation of the Coastliner service in 1995. The eastern section of that service, between Rhyl and Chester, is now marketed as Mainline Seaside and Deeside. Optare Vecta-bodied MAN SMM504, M504AJC, is seen at Chester bus exchange in April. *Tom Johnson*

Once prevalent throughout the Crosville area was the lightweight Leyland National B-series model produced by Leyland as a replacement for the Bristol LH. The model looked similar to the short National though much of the refinements, including the heating and ventilation systems and much sound proofing were removed. Still in the fleet is SNL572, JTU572T displaying Alpine Bus names on its red and white livery as it leaves Llandudno for Rhyl. *John Jones*

Apart from a pair of Iveco TurboDaily minibuses new in 1994, the Crosville Cymru minibus fleet are now of Mercedes-Benz manufacture. The latest examples have Alexander Sprint bodies on 709 or the larger 811 models. One of the latter is MMM718, N718DJC, pictured here in Llandudno.
Tony Wilson

Minibuses:

MMM33-46
Mercedes-Benz L608D   Alexander AM   B20F   1986   Ex Hastings & District, 1987

33	D433UHC	36	D436UHC	39	D439UHC	42	D442UHC	45	D445UHC
34	D434UHC	37	D437UHC	40	D440UHC	43	D443UHC	46	D446UHC
35	D435UHC	38	D438UHC	41	D441UHC	44	D444UHC		

MMM56-68
Mercedes-Benz L608D   Reeve Burgess   B20F   1986   Ex Hastings & District, 1987

56	D956UDY	59	D959UDY	62	D962UDY	65	D965UDY	67	D967UDY
58	D958UDY	60	D960UDY	63	D963UDY	66	D966UDY	68	D968UDY

MMM79-99
Mercedes-Benz L608D   Reeve Burgess   B20F*   1986-87 *99 is DP19F

79	D79VCC	84	D84VCC	88	D88VCC	91	D91VCC	96	D96VCC
80	D80VCC	85	D85VCC	89	D89VCC	92	D92VCC	98	D98VCC
81	D81VCC	86	D86VCC	90	D90VCC	94	D94VCC	99	D99VCC
82	D82VCC	87	D87VCC						

MMM153-191
Mercedes-Benz L608D   Alexander AM   B20F*   1986   Ex Milton Keynes Citybus, 1988
*173 is DP19F

153	D153VRP	169	D169VRP	172	D172VRP	175	D175VRP	189	D189VRP
154	D154VRP	170	D170VRP	173	D173VRP	182	D182VRP	191	D191VRP
167	D167VRP	171	D171VRP	174	D174VRP	188	D188VRP		

MMM202-207
Mercedes-Benz L608D   Reeve Burgess   B20F   1986   Ex London Country NW, 1988

202	C302SPL	203	C303SPL	204	C304SPL	206	C306SPL	207	C307SPL

MMM210-228
Mercedes-Benz 709D   Robin Hood   DP25F   1988-89

210	F210DCC	214	F214DCC	218	F218DCC	222	F222DCC	226	F426EJC
211	F211DCC	215	F215DCC	219	F219DCC	223	F223DCC	227	F427EJC
212	F212DCC	216	F216DCC	220	F220DCC	224	F424EJC	228	F428EJC
213	F213DCC	217	F217DCC	221	F221DCC	225	F425EJC		

MMM229-240	Mercedes-Benz 709D	Robin Hood	DP25F	1989	

229	G229FJC	233	G233FJC	235	G235FJC	237	G237FJC	239	G239FJC
230	G230FJC	234	G234FJC	236	G236FJC	238	G238FJC	240	G240FJC
232	G232FJC								

MMM241	G241GCC	Mercedes-Benz 709D	Phoenix	DP25F	1989	
MMM242	G242GCC	Mercedes-Benz 709D	Phoenix	DP25F	1989	
MMM243	G243GCC	Mercedes-Benz 709D	Phoenix	DP25F	1989	
MMM260	G160YRE	Mercedes-Benz 709D	LHE	B29F	1989	Ex Stevensons, 1994
MMM261	G161YRE	Mercedes-Benz 709D	LHE	B29F	1989	Ex Stevensons, 1994
MMM262	G162YRE	Mercedes-Benz 709D	LHE	B29F	1989	Ex Stevensons, 1994
MMM263	G163YRE	Mercedes-Benz 709D	LHE	B29F	1989	Ex Stevensons, 1994
MIF290	M290AJC	Iveco TurboDaily 59-12	Marshall C31	B27F	1994	
MIF291	M291AJC	Iveco TurboDaily 59-12	Marshall C31	B27F	1994	
MMM335	L35OKV	Mercedes-Benz 811D	Wright	B33F	1993	
MMM336	L36OKV	Mercedes-Benz 811D	Wright	B33F	1993	
MMM337	L37OKV	Mercedes-Benz 811D	Wright	B33F	1993	
MMM338	L38OKV	Mercedes-Benz 811D	Wright	B33F	1993	

MMM351-377	Mercedes-Benz 709D	Reeve Burgess Beaver	DP25F	1989	

351	G151FJC	370	G170FJC	372	G172FJC	374	G174FJC	376	G176FJC
352	G152FJC	371	G171FJC	373	G173FJC	375	G175FJC	377	G177FJC
369	G169FJC								

MMM411	M411BEY	Mercedes-Benz 811D	Alexander Sprint	B33F	1995	
MMM412	M412BEY	Mercedes-Benz 811D	Alexander Sprint	B33F	1995	
MMM413	M413BEY	Mercedes-Benz 811D	Alexander Sprint	B33F	1995	
MMM701	F701KMA	Mercedes-Benz 709D	Reeve Burgess Beaver	B27F	1989	Ex Midland, 1995
MMM702	F702KMA	Mercedes-Benz 709D	Reeve Burgess Beaver	B27F	1989	Ex Midland, 1995
MMM704	F704KMA	Mercedes-Benz 709D	Reeve Burgess Beaver	B27F	1989	Ex Midland, 1995
MMM711	M711YJC	Mercedes-Benz 709D	Marshall C19	B25F	1994	
MMM712	M712YJC	Mercedes-Benz 709D	Marshall C19	B25F	1994	
MMM713	M713YJC	Mercedes-Benz 709D	Marshall C19	B25F	1994	
MMM714	M714YJC	Mercedes-Benz 709D	Marshall C19	B25F	1994	
MMM715	L715WCC	Mercedes-Benz 709D	Marshall C19	B27F	1993	
MMM716	L716WCC	Mercedes-Benz 709D	Marshall C19	B27F	1993	
MMM717	L717WCC	Mercedes-Benz 709D	Marshall C19	B27F	1993	
MMM718	N718DJC	Mercedes-Benz 811D	Alexander Sprint	B33F	1995	
MMM719	N719DJC	Mercedes-Benz 811D	Alexander Sprint	B33F	1995	

MMM793-797	Mercedes-Benz 709D	Alexander Sprint	B27F	1995	

793	N993CCC	794	N994CCC	795	N995CCC	796	N996CCC	797	N997CCC

Some of the more distant midibus operations use the LHE-bodied example acquired from Stevensons in 1994 when only five years old. MMM260, G160YRE shows its rounded lines as it leaves Bangor, the building of the university visible in the background. *Tony Wilson*

Despite the recent acquisition of eight Leyland Olympians from Kentish Bus, the Bristol VRT remains by far the principal double-deck bus in the Crosville Cymru fleet. DVG518, YMB518W, is seen approaching Aberystwyth rail station before beginning the long journey along Cardigan Bay.
John Jones

Double Deck Vehicles:

EVG49	UVT49X	Bristol VRT/SL3/6LXB	Eastern Coach Works	DPH41/29F	1981	Ex Midland Fox, 1992	
EVG50	PFA50W	Bristol VRT/SL3/6LXB	Eastern Coach Works	DPH41/29F	1980	Ex Midland Fox, 1992	
OAL108	OCO108S	Leyland Atlantean AN68A/1R	Roe	O43/30F	1978	Ex Bee Line, 1993	
ODL190	JTD390P	Daimler Fleetline CRL6-33	Northern Counties	O49/29F	1975	Ex Southend, 1993	
DOG191	B191BLG	Leyland Olympian ONLXB/1R	Eastern Coach Works	H45/32F	1985	Ex Crosville, 1986	
DOG192	B192BLG	Leyland Olympian ONLXB/1R	Eastern Coach Works	H45/32F	1985	Ex Crosville, 1986	
DOG193	B193BLG	Leyland Olympian ONLXB/1R	Eastern Coach Works	H45/32F	1985	Ex Crosville, 1986	
DOG194	B194BLG	Leyland Olympian ONLXB/1R	Eastern Coach Works	H45/32F	1985	Ex Crosville, 1986	
ODL195	JTD395P	Daimler Fleetline CRL6-33	Northern Counties	O49/29F	1976	Ex Southend, 1993	
DOG196	B196BLG	Leyland Olympian ONLXB/1R	Eastern Coach Works	H45/32F	1985	Ex Crosville, 1986	

EOG208-212		Leyland Olympian ONLXB/1R	Eastern Coach Works	DPH42/29F	1985	Ex Crosville, 1986

208	C208GTU	209	C209GTU	210	C210GTU	211	C211GTU	212	C212GTU

DOG220-232		Leyland Olympian ONLXB/1R	Eastern Coach Works	H45/32F*	1983	Ex Kentish Bus, 1995
						*220 is H44/32F

220	WDC220Y	222	AEF222Y	229	AEF229Y	230	CEF230Y	232	CEF232Y
221	AEF221Y	224	AEF224Y						

DOG258	C258UAJ	Leyland Olympian ONLXB/1R	Eastern Coach Works	H45/32F	1985	Ex Kentish Bus, 1995
DVL378	FTU378T	Bristol VRT/SL3/501	Eastern Coach Works	H43/31F	1978	Ex Crosville, 1986
DVL403	JMB403T	Bristol VRT/SL3/501	Eastern Coach Works	H43/31F	1978	Ex Crosville, 1987
DVL412	ODM412V	Bristol VRT/SL3/501	Eastern Coach Works	H43/31F	1979	Ex Crosville, 1987
DVL414	ODM414V	Bristol VRT/SL3/501	Eastern Coach Works	H43/31F	1979	Ex Midland Red North, 1993
DVL415	ODM415V	Bristol VRT/SL3/501	Eastern Coach Works	H43/31F	1979	Ex Midland Red North, 1993
DVL416	ODM416V	Bristol VRT/SL3/501	Eastern Coach Works	H43/31F	1979	Ex C-Line, 1993
DVL426	RLG426V	Bristol VRT/SL3/501	Eastern Coach Works	H43/27F	1980	Ex Crosville, 1986
OVL429	RLG429V	Bristol VRT/SL3/501	Eastern Coach Works	O43/27F	1980	Ex Crosville, 1991
DVL433	RMA433V	Bristol VRT/SL3/501	Eastern Coach Works	H43/31F	1980	Ex Crosville, 1986
DVL440	RMA440V	Bristol VRT/SL3/501	Eastern Coach Works	H43/31F	1980	Ex Crosville, 1986

After more than thirty years the limited stop Cymru Coastliner service from Caernarfon to Chester was withdrawn by Crosville Cymru during 1995. EOG210, C210GTU is one of five remaining Leyland Olympians with Eastern Coachworks bodywork and high-back seating, it is seen at Llandudno in April 1996 after a repaint into bus livery. *Tony Wilson*

DVG445-478   Bristol VRT/SL3/6LXB   Eastern Coach Works   H43/31F* 1980-81 Ex Crosville, 1986
*467/78 are O43/31F (prefix OVG) and ex Midland 1994

445	UDM445V	449	UDM449V	462	VCA462W	468	WTU468W	476	WTU476W
446	UDM446V	451	UDM451V	466	WTU466W	469	WTU469W	477	WTU477W
447	UDM447V	459	VCA459W	467	WTU467W	475	WTU475W	478	WTU478W

DVG500-534   Bristol VRT/SL3/6LXB   Eastern Coach Works   H43/31F* 1981   Ex Crosville, 1986
*512/9/28 are O43/31F (prefix OVG); 519/20 are ex Midland, 1994

500	YMB500W	506	YMB506W	514	YMB514W	521	BMA521W	529	DCA529X
501	YMB501W	507	YMB507W	516	YMB516W	522	BMA522W	530	DCA530X
502	YMB502W	510	YMB510W	517	YMB517W	524	BMA524W	532	DCA532X
503	YMB503W	511	YMB511W	518	YMB518W	525	DCA525X	533	DCA533X
504	YMB504W	512	YMB512W	519	YMB519W	527	DCA527X	534	DCA534X
505	YMB505W	513	YMB513W	520	BMA520W	528	DCA528X		

DVL598	BTU368S	Bristol VRT/SL3/501	Eastern Coach Works	H39/31F	1978	Ex SUT, 1989
OVG961	YCU961T	Bristol VRT/SL3/6LXB	Eastern Coach Works	O43/31F	1979	Ex Northumbria, 1994

Previous Registrations:

FAZ3193	C247SPC	HIL7592	E179FFT	SIB8583	A142EPA
FAZ3194	C250SPC	HIL7593	E180FFT	SIB9492	A149EPA
FAZ5181	A147EPA	SIB7689	C251SPC	YCU961T	OBR774T, WSV571

Livery: Green and white; green and yellow (Bws Gwynedd)

D & G COACHES

D O Brotherton, 3 Llwyn Bleddyn Road, Rachub, Llanllechid, Gwynedd, LL57 3EF

UDW137S	Leyland Leopard PSU4E/2R	Duple Dominant	B47F	1978	Ex Red & White, 1993
MFV32T	Leyland Leopard PSU4E/4R	East Lancashire	B47F	1978	Ex Burnley & Pendle, 1996
KGD778T	Volvo B58-56	Plaxton Supreme IV	C53F	1979	Ex Fulcher, Cheadle Hulme, 1995
RNY305Y	Leyland Tiger TRCTL11/2R	Plaxton Paramount 3200 E	C49F	1983	Ex Midland, Auchterarder, 1994
A860KFP	Volvo B10M-61	Plaxton Paramount 3200	C53F	1983	Ex Colins Coaches, Shepshed, 1994
C324LDT	Volvo B9M	Plaxton Paramount 3200 II	C43F	1986	Ex Airport Parking, Copthorne, 1995
D154LTA	Renault-Dodge S56	Reeve Burgess	DP23F	1986	Ex Dawson, Heywood, 1995
L261VSU	Mercedes-Benz 609D	Onyx	C24F	1994	

Livery: White and blue

The latest addition to the D&G fleet is this East Lancashire-bodied Leyland Leopard, MFV32T, seen at Talybont, near Bangor. It joins the former Red & White Leopard as a regular on the Bangor to Gerlan service 66 which, with the 65, Bangor - Bethesda, Llanrwst service forms the core of the D&G operation. *Ralph Stevens*

The North & West Wales Bus Handbook

DAVIES BROS

Davies Brothers (Pencader) Ltd, Blossom Garage, Pencader, Carmarthenshire, SA39 9HA
Davies Brothers (Carmarthen) Ltd, Abergwili Road Garage,
Carmarthen, Carmarthenshire, SA31 2HG

Depots :Blossom Garage, Pencader; Abergwili Road Garage, Carmarthen; Eynon's Garage, Heol Waunyclun, Trimsaran

85	NTH119H	Leyland Leopard PSU3A/4R	Plaxton Derwent	B60F	1970	
88	PTH408K	Leyland Leopard PSU3B/4R	Plaxton Elite	C53F	1971	
93	XBX650M	Leyland Leopard PSU3B/4R	Duple Dominant	DP53F	1974	
100	LBX861P	Leyland Leopard PSU3C/4R	Plaxton Supreme Express	C53F	1976	
107	HPT324H	Leyland Leopard PSU3A/4R	Plaxton Derwent	B55F	1970	Ex Dan Jones, Carmarthen, 1978
112	VTH888L	Leyland Leopard PSU3B/4R	Plaxton Elite III	C53F	1973	Ex Dan Jones, Carmarthen 1978
123	WBX1T	Leyland Leopard PSU3E/4R	Duple Dominant II	C53F	1979	
124	YBX917V	Leyland Leopard PSU3E/4R	Duple Dominant II	C53F	1979	
133	8124DD	Leyland Tiger TRCTL11/2R	Plaxton Supreme VI Express	C49F	1982	
146	1923DD	Leyland Tiger TRCTL11/3RH	Duple Laser	C57F	1984	
149	AKM433K	Leyland Leopard PSU4A/2R	Willowbrook	B52F	1971	Ex Farmer, Kennington 1985
150	TBX713	Leyland Leopard PSU3C/2R	Willowbrook Warrior (1988)	B53F	1976	Ex Lancaster, 1985
151	3475DD	Leyland Leopard PSU5C/4R	Plaxton Supreme V	C57F	1982	Ex Martindale Ferryhill, 1985
152	7289DD	Leyland Leopard PSU5C/4R	Duple Dominant II	C57F	1979	Ex Grey-Green, Stamford Hill, 1985

Shortly after the previous edition of the Welsh Bus Handbook was published service changes in
Dyfed saw Davies Bros regain much of the work it had lost earlier to SWT, especially in the
Carmarthen area. Seen in Lammas Street, Carmarthen is long-serving member of the fleet, 149,
AKM433K. *Malc McDonald*

153	MFR304P	Leyland Leopard PSU3C/2R	Alexander AYS	B53F	1976	Ex Lancaster, 1985
154	MFR302P	Leyland Leopard PSU3C/2R	Alexander AYS	B53F	1976	Ex Lancaster, 1985
155	3338DD	Leyland Tiger TRCTL11/3RZ	Duple Laser 2	C57F	1986	
156	7660DD	Leyland Tiger TRCTL11/3RZ	Plaxton Paramount 3500 II	C51FT	1987	
157	6690DD	Volvo B10M-53	Plaxton Paramount 4000 II	CH53/9DT	1987	*SOLD*
158	XTH333	Leyland Leopard PSU3C/4R	Willowbrook Warrior (1988)	B53F	1976	Ex Roberts, Aberystwyth, 1985
161	2405DD	Leyland Tiger TRCTL11/3RZ	Plaxton Paramount 3500 II	C53F	1987	
162	FEK1F	Leyland Leopard PSU3E/4R	Plaxton Supreme IV Express	C53F	1980	Ex Cream Line, Tonmawr, 1987
163	MBX447	Leyland Leopard PSU3C/4R	Willowbrook Warrior (1989)	B53F	1975	Ex Cream Line, Tonmawr, 1987
165	8098DD	Leyland Tiger TRCTL11/3R	Duple 340	C53FT	1987	
168	8853DD	Leyland Tiger TRCL10/3RZM	Duple 340	C53FT	1988	
170	5519DD	Leyland Leopard PSU4B/4R	Willowbrook Warrior (1988)	B45F	1973	Ex Hills, Tredegar, 1988 *SOLD*
171	UCK500	Leyland Leopard PSU4B/4RT	Willowbrook Warrior (1989)	B45F	1974	Ex National Welsh, 1988
175	WJF378S	AEC Reliance 6U3ZR	Duple Dominant II Express	DP53F	1978	Ex Eynons, Trimsaran, 1988 *SCRAP*
183	HCS793N	Leyland Leopard PSU3/3R	Alexander AYS	B53F	1975	Ex Eynons, Trimsaran, 1988 *SOLD*
199	F612RBX	Leyland Tiger TRCTL11/3RZ	Duple 340	C55F	1988	
200	5210DD	Leyland Tiger TRCL10/3ARZM	Plaxton Paramount 3500 III	C51FT	1988	
201	9616DD	Leyland Tiger TRCL10/3ARZM	Duple 340	C53FT	1988	
202	OUT11W	Leyland Leopard PSU3E/4R	Plaxton Supreme IV Express	C53F	1981	Ex Cottrells, Mitcheldean, 1988
204	D401SGS	Freight Rover Sherpa	Dormobile	B16F	1987	Ex Luton & District, 1988
207	D350KVA	Freight Rover Sherpa	Dormobile	B16F	1986	Ex Westward Travel, Hayle, 1988
208	GDE371W	Leyland Leopard PSU5D/4R (TL11)	Plaxton Supreme IV	C57F	1981	Ex Yorkshire Rider, 1988
209	FIL7131	Leyland Leopard PSU3B/4R	Willowbrook Warrior (1989)	B53F	1975	Ex Rover Coaches, Horsley, 1989
212	F113UBX	Leyland Tiger TRCTL11/3RZM	Plaxton Paramount 3500 III	C57F	1989	
214	F114UBX	Leyland Tiger TRCTL11/3ARZ	Duple 340	C53FT	1989	
215	GKK158V	Leyland Leopard PSU3E/4R	Willowbrook 003	DP49F	1979	Ex Maidstone & District, 1989 *SCRAP*
217	GKK157V	Leyland Leopard PSU3E/4R	Willowbrook 003	DP49F	1979	Ex Maidstone & District, 1989 *SCRAP*
220	UKG423S	Leyland Leopard PSU3E/2R	Willowbrook	B51F	1978	Ex Ffoshelig Motors, Newchurch, 1994
221	UKG474S	Leyland Leopard PSU4E/2R	Willowbrook	B45F	1978	Ex Inter Valley Link, 1989
222	UKG475S	Leyland Leopard PSU4E/2R	Willowbrook	B45F	1978	Ex Inter Valley Link, 1989
223	G304YBX	Mercedes-Benz 609D	Whittaker	C20F	1989	
228	A71VTX	Leyland Tiger TRBTL11/1R	East Lancashire	DP43F	1984	Ex National Welsh, 1989
229	A115UDE	Leyland Tiger TRCTL11/3L	Willowbrook Warrior (1990)	B51F	1984	Ex VL Bus, 1990
230	G36BBX	DAF MB230LT615	Plaxton Paramount 3500 III	C49FT	1990	
231	H595EBX	Volvo B10M-60	Van Hool Alizée	C49FT	1990	
232	H879EBX	Mercedes-Benz 709D	Dormobile Routemaker	B27F	1990	*ACCIDENT W/O*
233	H880EBX	Mercedes-Benz 709D	Dormobile Routemaker	B27F	1990	
234	H881EBX	Mercedes-Benz 709D	Dormobile Routemaker	B27F	1990	
235	G51OUB	Mercedes-Benz 709D	Dormobile Routemaker	B29F	1990	Ex Derwent, Leeds, 1990
236	LFT89X	Leyland Leopard PSU3F/4R	Willowbrook 003	C57F	1981	Ex Go-Ahead Northern, 1991 *SCRAP*
237	E976LBK	Iveco Daily 49-10	Robin Hood City Nippy	B25F	1988	Ex Horsham Buses, 1992
238	K499RBX	Volvo B10M-60	Jonckheere Deauville P599	C51FT	1992	
239	2358DD	Leyland Tiger TRCTL11/3ARZ	Plaxton P3200 III (1992)	C57F	1992	Ex VL Bus, 1991
240	MIB657	Aüwaerter Neoplan N122/3	Aüwaerter Skyliner	CH57/20CT	1985	Ex The Kings Ferry, 1993 *SOLD*
242	K182RBX	Renault Master T35D	Cymric	M16	1993	*SOLD*
243	L458VBX	Volvo B10M-60	Jonckheere Deauville P599	C51FT	1993	
244	H61WNN	Mercedes-Benz 709D	Scott	DP29F	1990	Ex Skills, Nottingham, 1993
245	L478WBX	Volvo B10M-60	Van Hool Alizée	C53FT	1994	
246	G63SNN	Mercedes-Benz 709D	Carlyle	DP29F	1990	Ex Skills, Nottingham, 1993
247	JLJ109V	Leyland Leopard PSU3E/4R	Plaxton Supreme IV Express	C53F	1980	Ex Yellow Buses, 1994
248	ERU108V	Leyland Leopard PSU3E/4R	Plaxton Supreme IV	C51F	1979	Ex Yellow Buses, 1994
249	ERU390V	Leyland Leopard PSU3E/4R	Plaxton Supreme IV Express	C53F	1979	Ex Yellow Buses, 1994
250	ADU327X	Leyland Tiger TRCTL11/3R	Plaxton Supreme V	C53F	1981	Ex Tellings-Golden Miller, Cardiff, 1994
251	E209KCK	Renault-Dodge S46	Northern Counties	B24F	1988	Ex Little White Buses, Ormskirk, 1995
252	M252CDE	Mercedes-Benz 709D	Mellor	B27F	1994	
253	M253CDE	Mercedes-Benz 811D	Mellor	B31F	1994	
254	M254CDE	Mercedes-Benz 811D	Mellor	B31F	1994	
255	M255CDE	Mercedes-Benz 811D	Mellor	B31F	1994	
256	M256CDE	Mercedes-Benz 811D	Mellor	B31F	1994	
257	M257CDE	Mercedes-Benz 811D	Mellor	B31F	1994	
258	M258CDE	Mercedes-Benz 811D	Mellor	DP31F	1994	
259	M259CDE	Mercedes-Benz 811D	Mellor	DP31F	1994	
260	M260VEJ	Dennis Dart 9.8SDL3040	East Lancashire	B43F	1995	*SOLD*

Opposite top: **Davies Bros. fleet contains several Leyland Leopards and one Tiger that have been re-bodied by Willowbrook between 1988 and 1990. One of the Leopards, 150, TBX713 was new to Lancaster as MFR301P and is seen arriving in Carparthen. The original body was an Alexander Y-type service bus.** *Malc MacDonald*

Opposite bottom: **While Mercedes-Benz is the current choice of minibus for Davies Bros., the requirement for midi buses led to the delivery of a Dennis Dart, 260, M260VEJ. The Dart is now quite common in Wales, but only two examples carry East Lancashire bodywork, the other being with Silcox.** *Tony Moyes*

The Ministry of Defence has regularly purchased large quantities of buses and coaches to fulfil a range of functions. Many of the coaches used for troop movements have secondary roles as ambulances in times of conflict. As such additional features do not comply to the stricter requirements of PCV licensing, though modifications can be made. Davies Bros purchased four such buses in 1995 and so far two have entered service, including A49VDE seen here. The other two will enter service in due course.

No.	Reg	Chassis	Body	Seats	Year	Notes
261	F721ENE	Leyland Tiger TRCTL11/3ARZM	Plaxton Paramount 3200 III	C53F	1988	Ex Shearings, 1995
262	F726ENE	Leyland Tiger TRCTL11/3ARZM	Plaxton Paramount 3200 III	C53F	1988	Ex Shearings, 1995
263	A36VDE	Leyland Tiger TRCTL11/3R	Marshall Campaigner	DP54F	1983	Ex MoD, 1995
264	N264HBX	DAF DE33WSSB3000	Van Hool Alizée	C51FT	1995	
265	D141LTA	Renault-Dodge S56	Reeve Burgess	B25F	1986	Ex Diamond-Glantawe, Morriston, 1996
266	D159LTA	Renault-Dodge S56	Reeve Burgess	B25F	1986	Ex Diamond-Glantawe, Morriston, 1996
267	D169LTA	Renault-Dodge S56	Reeve Burgess	B25F	1986	Ex Diamond-Glantawe, Morriston, 1996
268	A49VDE	Leyland Tiger TRCTL11/3R	Marshall Campaigner	DP54F	1983	Ex MoD, 1995
	20KB43	Leyland Tiger TRCTL11/3R	Marshall Campaigner	DP54F	1983	Ex MoD, 1995
	20KB79	Leyland Tiger TRCTL11/3R	Marshall Campaigner	DP54F	1983	Ex MoD, 1995

(handwritten note left margin: 6690DD, MIB657)

Previous Registrations:

1923DD	from new	8098DD	D615HBX	FEK1F	GCY124W
2358DD	A171UDE	8124DD	KBX78X	FIL7131	HNU117N
2405DD	from new	8853DD	E237MBX	GDE371W	LHE256W,2358DD
3338DD	from new	9616DD	F613RBX	MBX447	MUS104P
3475DD	SPY374X	A36VDE	20KB59	MIB657	IKOV,B662GWF
5210DD	F614RBX	A49VDE	20KB64	TBX713	MFR303P
5519DD	FWO154L	A..VDE	20KB43	UCK500	RBO194M
6690DD	D388FBX	A..VDE	20KB79	XTH333	OGR653P
7289DD	YYL774T, 6038DD	ADU327X	GNP111X, 26GJH, LWP947X, DJI2517		
7660DD	from new				

Livery: White, red and orange

The gains in Bws Dyfed contracts in 1994 saw a large influx of vehicles including eight new Mercedes-Benz minibuses and a Dennis Dart. These all meet Dyfed's interpretation of DpTAC specifications and Mellor built the bodies for these Mercedes-Benz as well as some for Silcox and Ffoshelig. Two of Davies' were fitted with high-back seats including M258CDE, seen here departing Llandyssul school.

To replace three Freight Rover Sherpas purchased second-hand in 1988-89 a trio of Renault-Dodge S56, which were new to Plymouth Citybus, were acquired early in 1996. They had been made redundant at Diamond-Glantawe on the sale of their bus services to SWT. First into service after refurbishment and repainting was 265, D141LTA. *John Jones*

DEVAWAY

B Randall, Broughton Mills Road, Bretton, Flintshire, CH4 0BY

Depots: Coed Talon Station, Pontybodkin; Rossbank Road, Ellesmere Port

3	CKC928X	Leyland National 2 NL116AL11/1R		B52F	1982	Ex Halton, 1996
4	HED203V	Leyland National 2 NL116L11/1R		B52F	1980	Ex Halton, 1996
14	EUM894T	Leyland National 11351A/1R		B49F	1979	Ex West Riding, 1991
15	PWW713R	Leyland National 11351A/1R		B52F	1976	Ex Yorkshire Woollen, 1989
16	PWW715R	Leyland National 11351A/1R		B52F	1976	Ex Yorkshire Woollen, 1989
19	EUM891T	Leyland National 11351A/1R		B49F	1977	Ex West Riding, 1990
23	D574VBV	Freight Rover Sherpa	Dormobile	B16F	1986	Ex Ribble, 1988
25	D580VBV	Freight Rover Sherpa	Dormobile	B16F	1986	Ex West, Woodford Green, 1988
31	E212PWY	Volkswagen LT55	Optare City Pacer	B25F	1987	Ex Lancaster, 1993
32	E213PWY	Volkswagen LT55	Optare City Pacer	B25F	1987	Ex Lancaster, 1993
33	E216PWY	Volkswagen LT55	Optare City Pacer	B25F	1987	Ex Lancaster, 1993
35	F414KHR	Volkswagen LT55	Optare City Pacer	DP25F	1988	Ex Lancaster, 1993

Revised services at the end of 1995 saw a reduction in fleet requirement allowing the older Leyland Nationals and Leopards to be withdrawn. Still operating are four of five Optare CityPacers which came from Lancaster in 1993. Odd one out, being fitted with high-back seats, is F414KHR, seen here in Chester. *Ralph Stevens*

74	PWT274W	Leyland Leopard PSU3E/4R	Willowbrook 003	C49F	1981	Ex West Yorkshire, 1988
88	RUA461W	Bristol VRT/SL3/6LXB	Eastern Coach Works	H43/31F	1981	Ex Yorkshire Woollen, 1994
89	JYG432V	Bristol VRT/SL3/6LXB	Eastern Coach Works	H43/31F	1979	Ex Yorkshire Woollen, 1994
90	JYG435V	Bristol VRT/SL3/6LXB	Eastern Coach Works	H43/31F	1980	Ex Yorkshire Woollen, 1994
92	RUA454W	Bristol VRT/SL3/6LXB	Eastern Coach Works	H43/31F	1981	Ex Yorkshire Woollen, 1994
93	RUA456W	Bristol VRT/SL3/6LXB	Eastern Coach Works	H43/31F	1981	Ex Yorkshire Woollen, 1994
94	KJO502W	Bristol VRT/SL3/6LXB	Eastern Coach Works	H43/27D	1980	Ex Oxford Bus Company, 1993
95	HUD495W	Bristol VRT/SL3/6LXB	Eastern Coach Works	H43/27D	1980	Ex Oxford Bus Company, 1993
96	HUD496W	Bristol VRT/SL3/6LXB	Eastern Coach Works	H43/27D	1980	Ex Oxford Bus Company, 1993
97	HUD501W	Bristol VRT/SL3/6LXB	Eastern Coach Works	H43/27D	1980	Ex Oxford Bus Company, 1993
98	HUD498W	Bristol VRT/SL3/6LXB	Eastern Coach Works	H43/27D	1980	Ex Oxford Bus Company, 1993
101	A101CVN	Ward Dalesman GRX1	Wadham Stringer Vanguard	B46D	1983	Ex Darlington, 1994
102	A102CVN	Ward Dalesman GRX1	Wadham Stringer Vanguard	B46D	1983	Ex Darlington, 1994
103	A103CVN	Ward Dalesman GRX1	Wadham Stringer Vanguard	B46D	1983	Ex Darlington, 1994
104	A104CVN	Ward Dalesman GRX1	Wadham Stringer Vanguard	B46D	1983	Ex Darlington, 1994
105	A105CVN	Ward Dalesman GRX1	Wadham Stringer Vanguard	B46D	1983	Ex Darlington, 1994
106	A106CVN	Ward Dalesman GRX1	Wadham Stringer Vanguard	B46D	1983	Ex Darlington, 1994

Livery: Cream and red

Eleven Bristol VRTs were acquired by Devaway around the time of the last edition of the book. The oldest has since been withdrawn for spares though the remainder, five from Oxford and five from West Riding's Yorkshire Woollen associate continue in service. The Yorkshire companies have since become subsidiaries of Crosville Cymru's parent, British Bus plc. JYG435V is seen in Chester.
Malc McDonald

EAGLES & CRAWFORD

J F, J K & W P Eagles & P Hughes, 53 New Street, Mold, Flintshire, CH7 1NY

1	OLG1V	Leyland Leopard PSU3E/4R	Plaxton Supreme IV	C53F	1979	
3	D143WCC	Freight Rover Sherpa	Carlyle	DP20F	1987	Ex Crosville Cymru, 1992
6	264ACA	Leyland Tiger TRCTL11/3R	Plaxton Paramount 3500 III	C53F	1984	Ex Derby, 1989
7	G258EHD	DAF SB2305DHS585	Duple 340	C57F	1989	Ex BAA, Gatwick, 1993
10	H168DJU	Toyota Coaster HB31R	Caetano Optimo	C21F	1990	
	F363MUT	Toyota Coaster HB31R	Caetano Optimo	C21F	1988	Ex Parkin, Rotherham, 1995
11	RLG292P	Bristol VRT/SL3/501	Eastern Coach Works	H43/31F	1976	Ex Crosville Cymru, 1990
	AHU512V	Bristol VRT/SL3/6LXB	Eastern Coach Works	H43/31F	1980	Ex City Line, 1994
14	YMB509W	Bristol VRT/SL3/6LXB	Eastern Coach Works	H43/31F	1981	Ex Crosville Cymru, 1991
	DSU772	Volvo B10M-61	Plaxton Paramount 3200 II	C53F	1985	Ex P&O Lloyd, Bagillt, 1995
15	E756HJF	Dennis Javelin 12SDA1907	Duple 320	C57F	1988	Ex Astley, Bury, 1991
16	RMA435V	Bristol VRT/SL3/501	Eastern Coach Works	H43/31F	1980	Ex Crosville Cymru, 1991

Previous Registrations:

264ACA	A444DTO		DSU772	B908SPR

Livery: White, blue and orange

Eagles and Crawford retain four double-deck buses for school services, three coming from Crosville Cymru, including the oldest, photographed in Mold, RLG292P. As with many Bristol VRTs with smaller operators in the area, the presentation of the vehicles belies their advancing years. Fleet numbers have not been allocated to recent arrivals. *John Jones*

EDWARDS BROS

R W Edwards, The Garage, Broad Haven Road, Tiers Cross, Haverfordwest, Pembrokeshire, SA62 3DA

WJB490	Leyland Leopard PSU3C/4R	Duple Dominant	C53F	1976	Ex Lewis, Whitland, 1991
BBR736S	Bedford YMT	Duple Dominant	B53F	1977	Ex Evans, Tregaron, 1996
OTR411S	Bedford YMT	Duple Dominant II	C53F	1977	Ex Evans, Tregaron, 1996
668VDE	Volvo B58-56	Plaxton Supreme III	C53F	1978	Ex Evans, Tregaron, 1992
OCX670X	Ford R1114	Duple Dominant IV	C53F	1981	Ex Walton, Cardiff, 1996
OWO235Y	Leyland Leopard PSU3G/2R	Duple Dominant	DP49F	1982	Ex Jones, Login, 1991
A200PCJ	Bedford YNT	Duple Laser	C53F	1983	Ex Evans, Tregoron, 1995
A734JAY	Volvo B10M-56	Plaxton Paramount 3200 E	C53F	1984	Ex Rover, Bromsgrove, 1991
B511TFO	Bedford CF	Steedrive Parflo	M12	1985	Ex Young, Newent, 1988
D570EWS	Freight Rover Sherpa	Dormobile	B16F	1986	Ex Badgerline, 1989
526NDE	Volvo B10M-61	Plaxton Paramount 3500 III	C51F	1987	Ex Vale of Llangollen, 1996
E677LDE	Freight Rover Sherpa	Made-to-Measure	DP16F	1987	Ex Jones, Login, 1994
E885MYP	Freight Rover Sherpa	Freight Rover	M16	1988	Ex private owner, 1992
E187DBB	Toyota Coaster HB31R	Caetano Optimo	C18F	1988	Ex Stones, Bath, 1992
E255PEL	Dennis Javelin 8.5SDL1903	Duple 320	C35F	1988	Ex Ashford Luxury Coaches, 1994
E333MDE	Dennis Javelin 11SDL1905	Duple 320	C53F	1988	
891VDE	Dennis Javelin 12SDA1907	Plaxton Paramount 3200 III	C55F	1988	Ex Ardenvale, Knowle, 1995
F383MUT	Mercedes-Benz 609D	Yeates	C24F	1988	
F130TRU	Mercedes-Benz L307D	Yeates	M12	1988	Ex Ciril Evans, Senghenydd, 1995
F567ABV	Freight Rover Sherpa	Elme Orion	B21F	1989	Ex Evans, Tregaron, 1992
M940CDE	LDV 400	LDV	M16	1995	
N50RDE	Dennis Javelin 12SDA2155	Plaxton Premiére 320	C53F	1996	

Previous Registrations:

3432RE	-	891VDE	E988KJF
526NDE	D290UDM, VLT290, VLT191, D328UTU	WJB490	NNW100P
668VDE	XWX197S, BYD90B		

Livery: Cream, tan and brown

Small-coach sales has been enhanced since the introduction of the Caetano Optimo-bodied Toyota Coaster to the British market. Until then, truck-derived solutions had some unfortunate qualities while minibus-based versions were somewhat cramped. Edwards Bros mark one version, E187DBB, is pictured at Tiers Cross. *John Jones*

Recently, Edwards Bros have acquired a new garage approximately 400 metres from their existing, rather cramped, premises in the centre of the village. The new facility accommodates an expanded fleet which, in addition to three Pembrokeshire contracts, Milford Haven and Haverfordwest town services, and a twice-weekly Dale/Marloes to Haverfordwest service runs several school and works contracts. Former Merthyr Tydfil Leopard OWO235Y is shown ready for service to Dale *(top)* while a new to Wallace Arnold Volvo B58, 668VDE *(bottom)* demonstrates the operator's keenness to acquire locally-issued, cherished marks. *Vernon Morgan*

ELLIS TRAVEL

F B Ellis, Church Street, Llangefni, Anglesey, LL77 7DU

VOD547K	Bristol VRT/SL2/6LX	Eastern Coach Works	H39/31F	1971	Ex South Midland, 1989
ATA556L	Bristol VRT/SL2/6LX	Eastern Coach Works	H43/32F	1973	Ex Western National, 1986
HRP674N	Bristol VRT/SL2/6LX	Eastern Coach Works	H43/31F	1975	Ex Pat's Coaches, New Broughton, 1990
SNJ684R	Bristol VRT/SL3/6LXB	Eastern Coach Works	H43/31F	1977	Ex Brighton & Hove, 1993
XYK747T	Bedford YMT	Duple Dominant II	C49F	1978	Ex Grey Green, Stamford Hill, 1982
VIA8311	Volvo B58-61	Plaxton Supreme III	C53F	1978	Ex Smith, High Wycombe, 1989
XDL304	Volvo B58-61	Plaxton Supreme IV	C51F	1979	Ex Regency, Portsmouth, 1986
HJP472V	Ford R1114	Duple Dominant II	C53F	1980	Ex Wilkinson, Hebburn, 1987
241KRO	Volvo B10M-61	Van Hool Alizée	C48FT	1981	Ex Reed, Kinsley, 1994
TIB4587	Leyland Tiger TRCTL11/3R	Plaxton Paramount 3500	C49F	1984	Ex Trumans, Pontypool, 1992
B440VOW	Mercedes-Benz L608D	Robin Hood	C25F	1985	Ex Aron, Northolt, 1988
PIB2734	Iveco Daily 49.10	Robin Hood City Nippy	B21F	1986	Ex Pickford, Grittleton, 1993
F368RPO	Iveco Daily 49.10	Robin Hood City Nippy	B23F	1989	Ex Robin Hood demonstrator, 1991
G121GOJ	Leyland DAF 400	Beadles	M16	1990	Ex Autoservices, Pontypool, 1993

Previous Registrations:

241KRO	NFJ380W	TIB4587	B488TYG	XDL304	EWW236T
PIB2734	C516DYM	VIA8311	ADF669T		

Livery: White, mauve and red (coaches); yellow, mushroom and red (buses)

Ellis' four Bristol VRTs are mostly to series 2 specification. HRP674N, which was new to United Counties, is a late example and was that operator's penultimate series 2 VR numerically. Changes to Gwynedd contracts in 1995 see Ellis now operating service 36 (Llangefni to Pencraig circular), 45 (Llangefni to Rhosneigr) and town service 48 ('The Llangefni Clipa'). *Brian West*

Empire Goldstar and its forerunner, Gold Star of St Asaph operated an extensive fleet of former Merseyside Fleetlines, up to two dozen being accumulated in the late 1980s. Only a handful remain now of which CKC327L is one. *Ralph Stevens*

Replacements for the Fleetlines have mostly been Bristol VRs, all with Eastern Coach Works bodies. The first to arrive was a former Trent example and the only series 2 of the half-dozen operated. Here PRR121L leads 'wing' of Empire double-deckers out on school duties, hopefully to the approval of their proprietor, a former RAF Officer. *Ralph Stevens*

EMPIRE GOLDSTAR

W O Blythin, Empire Coach Station, Tremarl, Llandudno Junction, Conwy LL31 9NF

Depots : Tremarl, Llandudno Junction and Hotpoint site, Bodelwyddan

CYG154H	Bristol LH6L	Plaxton Elite	C45F	1970	Ex Bassett's, Tittensor, 1993
OEY348J	Leyland Atlantean PDR2/1	Alexander L	H47/32D	1971	Ex Gold Star, St Asaph, 1992
GWY961J	Bristol LHL6L	Plaxton Elite	C51F	1971	Ex Bassett's, Tittensor, 1993
CKC301L	Daimler Fleetline CRG6LXB	MCW	H43/32F	1973	Ex Shearings, 1992
CKC304L	Daimler Fleetline CRG6LXB	MCW	H43/32F	1972	Ex Gold Star, St Asaph, 1992
CKC327L	Daimler Fleetline CRG6LXB	MCW	H43/32F	1973	Ex Gold Star, St Asaph, 1992
CKC336L	Daimler Fleetline CRG6LXB	MCW	H43/32F	1973	Ex Shearings, 1992
CKC343L	Daimler Fleetline CRG6LXB	MCW	H43/32F	1973	Ex Gold Star, St Asaph, 1992
PRR121L	Bristol VRT/SL2/6G	Eastern Coach Works	H39/31F	1973	Ex Happy Days, Woodseaves, 1993
NLJ521M	Bristol LH6L	Eastern Coach Works	B43F	1974	Ex Shearings, 1992
NLJ525M	Bristol LH6L	Eastern Coach Works	B43F	1974	Ex Shearings, 1992
LJT941P	Bristol LH6L	Eastern Coach Works	B43F	1975	Ex Shearings, 1992
LMA609P	Bristol LH6L	Eastern Coach Works	B43F	1975	Ex Bob the Garage, Llanddulas, 1992
OWE856R	Bristol VRT/SL3/501	Eastern Coach Works	H43/31F	1977	Ex Yellow Buses, 1995
RWA860R	Bristol VRT/SL3/501	Eastern Coach Works	H43/31F	1977	Ex Yellow Buses, 1995
RWE861R	Bristol VRT/SL3/501	Eastern Coach Works	H43/31F	1977	Ex Yellow Buses, 1995
TDT863S	Bristol VRT/SL3/501	Eastern Coach Works	H43/31F	1977	Ex Yellow Buses, 1995
OTC608R	Bristol LH6L	Eastern Coach Works	B43F	1977	Ex Lewis y Ilan, Amlwch, 1995
PCA419V	Bristol VRT/SL3/501	Eastern Coach Works	H43/31F	1979	Ex Liveley, Marple, 1994
1862HX	Leyland Leopard PSU5C/4R	Duple Dominant II	C57F	1980	Ex Shearings, 1992
FIL4161	Leyland Tiger TRCTL11/2R	Plaxton Paramount 3200E	C53F	1983	Ex Wardell, Prestatyn, 1993
B176WYV	Leyland Cub CU435	Wadham Stringer Vanguard	B32F	1984	Ex LB Lewisham, 1993
B183WYV	Leyland Cub CU435	Wadham Stringer Vanguard	B32F	1984	Ex White Lion, Tredegar, 1993
C523BFB	Ford Transit 190	Dormobile	B16F	1985	Ex Eagles & Crawford, Mold, 1994
546FJB	Volvo B10M-61	Van Hool Alizee	C53F	1986	Ex Shearings, 1992
984FJB	Volvo B10M-61	Van Hool Alizee	C53F	1986	Ex Shearings, 1992
610LYB	Volvo B10M-61	Plaxton Paramount 3500 III	C48FT	1988	Ex Caelloi, Pwllheli, 1995
428EJB	Dennis Javelin 11SDA1906	Duple 320	C51FT	1989	Ex County of Avon, 1994
G843HRN	Mercedes-Benz 609D	Reeve Burgess Beaver	B23F	1990	Ex Ratcliffe, Oswaldtwistle, 1992

Previous Registrations:

1862HX	XFR842V	610LYB	E909UNW	FIL4161	RNY308Y
428EJB	F906UPR	984FJB	C531DND	OEY348J	XKC792J, 984FJB
546FJB	C533DND				

Livery: Cream/white, yellow and orange

The current Empire Goldstar business was founded after Shearings sold their Llandudno operation, originally Gwalia Coaches. Several service buses from Gwalia were transferred, including four Bristol LH saloons with others added later, one of which, LMA609P, seen here at Tremarland, was a later arrival. The Empire Goldstar business was sold to Alpine in 1996.
Tony Moyles

EXPRESS MOTORS

E W & J A Jones, Gerallt, Bontnewydd, Caernarfon, Gwynedd, LL54 7VN

Depots :Llwyn Gelli Ind Est, Blaenau Ffestiniog and Llyfni Road, Pengroes.

u	604JPU	Bristol SC4LK	Eastern Coach Works	B35F	1957	Ex preservation, 1989
u	OVL494	Bristol SC4LK	Eastern Coach Works	B35F	1960	Ex preservation, 1989
w	TBD278G	Bristol RELH6G	Eastern Coach Works	DP49F	1969	Ex United Counties, 1987
w	TBD284G	Bristol RELH6G	Eastern Coach Works	DP49F	1969	Ex United Counties, 1986
	HHA183L	Leyland Leopard PSU4B/4R	Plaxton Elite III	C40F	1973	Ex Pilgrim, Southampton, 1987
	EXI2455	Ley National 1151/1R/2802 (Volvo)	E L Greenway (1993)	B49F	1973	Ex C&H, Fleetwood, 1993
	NPU982M	Bristol VRT/SL2/6LX	Eastern Coach Works	H39/31F	1973	Ex Eastern National, 1987
	MDS691P	Leyland Atlantean AN68A/1R	Alexander AL	H45/31F	1976	Ex R&M Coaches, Par, 1995
	YTU325S	Leyland Leopard PSU3E/4R	Duple Dominant I	DP49F	1977	Ex North Western, 1991
	EXI1726	Leyland Leopard PSU3E/4R	Willowbrook Warrior (1991)	B49F	1978	Ex RoadCar, 1991
	EMB369S	Leyland National 11351A/1R		B49F	1978	Ex Crosville Cymru, 1990
	AYG849S	Bristol VRT/SL3/6LXB	Eastern Coach Works	H43/31F	1978	Ex Keighley & District, 1990
	GMB382T	Leyland National 11351A/1R		B49F	1978	Ex Crosville Cymru, 1990
	GMB649T	Leyland National 10351B/1R		B44F	1978	Ex Crosville Cymru, 1990
w	UEY398T	Volvo B58-61	Plaxton Supreme IV	C44FT	1979	Ex Arvonia Llanrug, 1989
	GGE163T	Leyland National 10351A/1R		B41F	1979	Ex Dunn-Line, Nottingham, 1992
	OJC496	Volvo B58-56	Plaxton Supreme IV	C53F	1979	Ex Southern, Barrhead, 1987
	EXI790	DAF MB200DKTL550	Plaxton Supreme IV	C44F	1980	Ex Harris Coach, W Thurrock, 1991
➜	LIL7438	Mercedes-Benz L508D	Reeve Burgess	DP19F	1981	Ex PMT, 1995
	A80RGE	Mercedes-Benz L307D	Reeve Burgess	M12	1983	Ex Ross, Edinburgh, 1987
	8443PH	Van Hool T818	Van Hool Astromega	CH50/10DT	1983	Ex Martindale, Shildon, 1992
	C327PEW	Mercedes-Benz L307D	Reeve Burgess	M12	1986	Ex Premier Travel, 1990
	C441BHY	Ford Transit 190D	Dormobile	B16F	1986	Ex Cardiff Bluebird, 1995
	C454BHY	Ford Transit 190D	Dormobile	B16F	1986	Ex Varteg, Garndiffaith, 1991
	E566JFR	Leyland Swift LBM6T/2RS	Wadham Stringer Vanguard	B37F	1987	Ex Aintree Coachline, 1992
	F356TSX	Mercedes-Benz 609D	Alexander Sprint	B25F	1988	Ex Brown, East Kilbride, 1992
➜	G609JET	Mercedes-Benz 609D	Whittaker Europa	B20F	1989	Ex Formby Coaches, 1992
	G222EOA	Mercedes-Benz 811D	Carlyle	B31F	1989	Ex Jones, Blaenau Ffestiniog, 1992
	DAY1T	DAF MB200DTL615	Van Hool Alizée	C53F	1989	Ex North Kent Express, 1996

Previous Registrations:

8443PH	TOA747Y	EXI726	YVL564S	OJC496	LUS909V
DAY1T	F622HGO	EXI790	NEV774V	UEY398T	DAY1T
EXI2455	BCD801L	LIL7438	CSC818W		

Opposite top: **Willowbrook Warrior bodywork and a dateless index mark disguise the original identity of EXI1726. Originally the Leyland Leopard was acquired from RoadCar as YVL564S, its Duple coachwork being removed to give way to the Willowbrook product.** *Paul Wigan*
Opposite bottom: **One of the more unusual buses in the fleet is E566JFR, a Leyland Swift, this example fitted with Wadham Stringer Vanguard bodywork. It is seen in Caernarfon.** *Tony Moyes*

Express Motors have acquired a large depot in Pen-y-groes to replace the small yard at Bontnewydd. Pictured at the Express yard is former Strathclyde Leyland National GGE163T awaiting service on route 1, Blaenau Ffestiniog to Caernarfon through Porthmadog.
Brian West

FFOSHELIG COACHES

P R Evans, Maes-y-prior, Llysonnen Road, Carmarthenshire SA33 5DS

Depot: Ffoshelig Garage, Newchurch,

STT413R	Bristol LH6L	Eastern Coach Works	B43F	1977	Ex Ffoshelig Motors, 1996
XUY59V	Volvo B58-56	Plaxton Supreme IV Express	C53F	1980	Ex Ffoshelig Motors, 1996
KUY442X	Volvo B10M-56	Plaxton Supreme IV	C53F	1982	Ex Ffoshelig Motors, 1996
B665OFP	DAF SB2300DHS585	Plaxton Paramount 3200 II	C53F	1985	Ex Evans, Tregaron, 1996

Previous Registrations:
XUY59V   LRH809V,6261TW,HPY838V,MOI3565

Livery: Cream, and two-tone brown

June 1st 1996 saw the last day of operations for Ffoshelig Motors, owned by the Jones family for 75 years to the month. Many aspects of this highly respected operation will continue following the dispersal of the fleet locally. A new operator, Rhodri Evans, is retaining the depot and smart livery on his three vehicles. This study of former London Buses Bristol LH, OJD54R, serves to remind readers of the standards set by the retiring owners. *John Jones*

FISHER

W E, D & N G Fisher, Little Green, Bronington, Wrexham SY13 3HQ

Reg	Chassis	Body	Type	Year	History
NMS588M	Leyland Leopard PSU3/3R	Alexander AYS	B53F	1973	Ex Meredith, Malpas, 1987
UUX357S	Ford R1114	Plaxton Supreme III	C53F	1978	Ex Salopia, Whitchurch, 1982
HUX18V	Ford R1114	Plaxton Supreme IV Express	C53F	1980	
HUX20V	Ford R1114	Plaxton Supreme IV	C53F	1980	
LUA267V	Ford R1114	Plaxton Supreme IV	C53F	1980	Ex Woburn, Islington, 1983
VJU255X	Ford R1114	Plaxton Supreme V Express	C53F	1982	Ex Dave Parry, Cheslyn Hay, 1985
GUG929Y	Ford R1114	Plaxton Paramount 3200	C53F	1983	Ex Dalesman, Ilkley, 1988
A419XHL	Volvo B10M-56	Plaxton Paramount 3200	C53F	1983	Ex Harrod, Wormegay, 1989
A647GLD	Volvo B10M-61	Plaxton Paramount 3200	C51F	1984	Ex Capital, West Drayton, 1987
A36DTV	Volvo B10M-61	Van Hool Alizée	C53F	1984	Ex Skills, Sheffield, 1990
947JWD	Volvo B10M-61	Van Hool Alizée	C53F	1985	Ex Shearings, 1992
HSV674	Volvo B10M-61	Van Hool Alizée	C53F	1986	Ex Shearings, 1992
C27BPR	Ford Transit 190	Carlyle	B16F	1986	Ex SUT, 1989
C514DND	Volvo B10M-61	Plaxton Paramount 3200 II	C53F	1986	Ex Wilson's, Carnwath, 1994
D258HFX	Volvo B10M-61	Plaxton Paramount 3200 III	C53F	1987	Ex Woodstones, Kidderminster, 1993
E123RAX	Freight Rover Sherpa	Carlyle Citybus 2	B20F	1987	Ex Red & White, 1994
F595USG	Iveco Daily 49.10	Carlyle Dailybus 2	B25F	1988	Ex Trent, 1993
G873YDU	Toyota Coaster HB31R	Caetano Optimo	C21F	1990	Ex Supreme, Coventry, 1993

Previous Registrations:

947JWD	B475UNB	HSV674	C536DND

Livery: Cream/white and blue

Fisher's base business remains its one or two days per week service between Little Green/Bronington and Wrexham, Whitchurch and Shrewsbury as well as links between Whitchurch and Oswestry or Chester. As such much of the journey is in Cheshire with the Whitchurch to Chester link being a CheshireBus service. The fleet fits the current pattern of many similar operators, that is older and trusty lightweights supplemented by modern heavyweight coaches for longer distance work. Wallace Arnold subsidiary, Woburn Garages, was the source of this Plaxton-bodied Ford. LUA267V left the main Wallace Arnold fleet in 1981. *Tom Johnson*

The GHA Coaches has expanded steadily through the 1990s from a rural minibus operation to a significant player in the Wrexham area, over 30 kilometres to the east where a second base has been established. 1996 saw the arrival of the first new vehicles, a pair of Marshall-bodied Mercedes-Benz 709s. One, N2GHA, is seen on a damp spring morning in Wrexham. *Tom Johnson*

Opposite: GHA's first up-market coach arrived in 1993 in the form of this Leyland Royal Tiger Doyen. It was one of a pair of Roe-built Doyens new to the Scottish Bus Group subsidiary, Alexander Northern. *John Jones*

Now one of the longest serving vehicles in the GHA fleet D512NDA is a Freight Rover Sherpa with Dormobile shell converted by Carlyle. It was photographed passing through Corwen. *John Jones*

G H A COACHES

EL Davies and G & A Davies, Mill Garage, Bettws Gwerfil Goch, Corwen,
Denbighshire LL21 9PU

Depots : Mill Garage, Bettws Gwerfil Goch and Bersham Enterprise Centre, Rhostyllen, Wrexham.

URF660S	Bristol VRT/SL3/501	Eastern Coach Works	H43/31F	1977	Ex PMT, 1992
BTU364S	Bristol VRT/SL3/501	Eastern Coach Works	H43/31F	1978	Ex PMT, 1992
NLG833T	Bedford YMT	Duple Dominant II	C53F	1979	Ex Acton Coaches, Wrexham, 1993
YAX21T	Ford R1114	Duple Dominant II	C53F	1979	Ex Archway Motors, Towcester, 1991
BWJ68T	Bedford YLQ	Duple Dominant II	C45F	1979	Ex Llew Jones Coaches, Llanrwst, 1991
SGR792V	Bristol VRT/SL3/6LXB	Eastern Coach Works	H43/31F	1980	Ex Northumbria, 1995
DBX548W	Bedford YMQ	Duple Dominant II	C45F	1980	Ex Dyma-Fo, Coaches, 1988
YKS22W	Bedford YLQ	Plaxton Supreme IV Express	C45F	1980	Ex Munro, Jedburgh, 1991
ORA13W	Ford R1114	Plaxton Supreme IV	C53F	1981	Ex Lynx, Llansannan, 1995
WIB1701	Bedford YNT	Plaxton Paramount 3200	C53F	1983	Ex Luker, Crondall, 1994
A419FSA	Leyland Royal Tiger B54	Roe Doyen	C46FT	1984	Ex Ashall, Levenshulme, 1993
CIB7866	Leyland Tiger TRCTL11/3R	Plaxton Paramount 3500	C49FT	1983	Ex Sargeant's, Kington, 1995
C588ORG	Leyland Royal Tiger RT	Van Hool Alizée	C49FT	1986	Ex Aline, Pelaw, 1996
D512NDA	Freight Rover Sherpa	Carlyle	B18F	1986	Ex Hyndburn, 1991
D948UDY	Mercedes-Benz L608D	Alexander AM	DP19F	1986	Ex Red & White, 1996
D777JUB	Freight Rover Sherpa	Dormobile	B20F	1986	Ex Globe, Barnsley, 1994
E108OUH	Freight Rover Sherpa	Carlyle Citybus 2	B20F	1987	Ex Red & White, 1995
E112RAX	Freight Rover Sherpa	Carlyle Citybus 2	B18F	1987	Ex Red & White, 1995
E121RAX	Freight Rover Sherpa	Carlyle Citybus 2	B20F	1987	Ex Red & White, 1995
E312XGB	Mercedes-Benz 609D	North West Coach Sales	C24F	1987	Ex Globe, Barnsley, 1994
E150RNY	Freight Rover Sherpa	Carlyle Citybus 2	B20F	1988	Ex Red & White, 1995
G432YAY	Toyota Coaster HB31R	Caetano Optimo	C21F	1990	Ex Kestrel Mini Coaches, Luton, 1995
N2GHA	Mercedes-Benz 709D	Marshall C19	B27F	1996	
N3GHA	Mercedes-Benz 709D	Marshall C19	B27F	1996	

Previous Registrations:

CIB7866	ANA109Y	NLG833T	OCW840T, 8158DF
WIB1710	VGM244Y, 8466PH, NRV303Y, HSV343, CPE344Y		

Livery: Grey, red and maroon

George Edwards' two services, E10 Wrexham - Coedpoeth - Minera and E12, Wrexham - Coedpoeth - Bryngwyn are maintained by well presented Duple Dominant bus-bodied Bedfords, two of which have been acquired since the last edition of this book. An arrival from Rider York in 1993, C472LKU was photographed in Wrexham town centre in August two years later. *John Jones*

Goodsir have retained the service from Llaingoch to Treseifion through Holyhead under contract to Gwynedd County Council and accordingly adorned with Bws Gwynedd red front, H466LEY is seen preparing to take up service. *Malc McDonald*

GEORGE EDWARDS & SON

GF & G Edwards, Berwyn, Bwlchgwyn, Wrexham, LL11 5UE

A698AWB	Bedford YMT	Duple Dominant	B55F	1984	Ex Caelloi, Pwllheli, 1996
C472LKU	Bedford YMT	Duple Dominant	B55F	1986	Ex Rider York, 1993
D642DRT	Bedford YNT	Duple Dominant	B63F	1987	Ex Chambers, Bures, 1995
E370ECJ	Bedford YNT	Plaxton Paramount 3200 III	C53F	1987	
G256EHD	DAF MB230LB615	Van Hool Alizée	C55F	1989	Ex Hanmer, Southsea, 1986
G261EHD	DAF SB2305DHTD585	Plaxton Paramount 3200 III	C57F	1989	
G112JBO	Leyland Tiger TRCL10/3ARZM	Plaxton Paramount 3500 III	C49FT	1990	Ex Eagles & Crawford, Mold, 1994

Livery: Red, maroon and ivory

GOODSIR

W C Goodsir, 30 Trenwfa Road, Lands End, Holyhead, Anglesey LL65 1LE

SXA63K	Daimler Fleetline CRG6LXB	Alexander AD	H44/31F	1971	Ex Fife Scottish, 1986
HRE531N	Bristol VRT/SL2/6LX	Eastern Coach Works	H43/31F	1975	Ex PMT, 1990
BHO57R	Leyland Leopard PSU3C/4R	Duple Dominant	C53F	1977	Ex Meyric, Magor, 1987
798EYG	Leyland Leopard PSU5B/4R	Plaxton Viewmaster III	C50FT	1977	Ex Eagre, Gainsborough, 1989
BAZ7378	Leyland National 11351A/1R		B48F	1978	Ex Bajwa, Slough, 1995
SFO139S	Bedford YMT	Duple Dominant II	C53F	1978	Ex Ellis, Llangefni, 1989
JTU597T	Leyland National 10351B/1R		B44F	1979	Ex Jones Llanfaethlu, 1991
102UTF	Volvo B10M-61	Jonckheere Jubilee P50	C49FT	1983	Ex Oare's of Holywell, 1994
297EYR	Van Hool T815	Van Hool Alizée	C53FT	1983	Ex APT, Rayleigh, 1995
H466LEY	Mercedes-Benz 709D	Reeve Burgess Beaver	B25F	1991	

Previous Registrations:

102UTF	MRP847Y, NAG455A	297EYR	TRT182, 827APT, BJS98Y, APT42S, UJN995Y
BAZ7378	YCD85T	798EYG	TKM644R, 2160RE, VFE686R

Livery: White, black, yellow and orange or white

GREAT ORME TOURS

Conwy County Borough Council, Maesdu Road, Llandudno, Conwy LL30 1HF

4		Hurst Nelson	Hurst Nelson	ST48T	1902	
5		Hurst Nelson	Hurst Nelson	ST48T	1902	
6		Hurst Nelson	Hurst Nelson	ST48T	1903	
7		Hurst Nelson	Hurst Nelson	ST48T	1903	
	JC8344	Guy Wolf NLW	Barnards	B21F	1948	
	YHP760J	Bedford VAS5	Duple Vista	C29F	1971	Ex Windsorian, Windsor, 1977
	NPF650W	Bedford VAS5	Duple Dominant	C29F	1981	Ex Hassell, Delamere, 1993
	TFP12X	Bedford VAS5	Plaxton Supreme IV	C29F	1981	Ex Capitol, Pontypool, 1992
	A609XFM	Bedford VAS5	Plaxton Supreme IV	C29F	1984	Ex Barry Cooper, Stockton Heath, 1992

Previous Registrations:
A609XFM   A422KBA, UCE665

Livery: Blue and gold

GWYNFOR COACHES

G Hughes, Anwylfa, 1 Greenfield Avenue, Llangefni, Anglesey LL77 7NU

Depots : Greenfield Avenue, Llangefni and Gaerwen

	FWB494V	Bedford YLQ	Duple Dominant II	C45F	1980	Ex Lewis, Llanrhystyd, 1995
—	PIB2474	Volvo B10M-61	Van Hool Alizée	C51F	1983	Ex Sinclair, Greenhead, 1993
	E710GNH	Toyota Coaster HB31R	Caetano Optimo	C21F	1987	Ex Dale Hire, Astwood Bank, 1991
	E77LRN	Mercedes-Benz 407D	Reeve Burgess	M15	1988	Ex Cicely demonstrator, 1990
	F888CRN	Mercedes-Benz 814D	Reeve Burgess Beaver	C33F	1989	Ex Cicely demonstrator, 1990
	N10HDA	Mercedes-Benz 811D	Mellor	B31F	1995	

Previous Registrations:
PIB2474   ENF577Y, YTP749, GNF477Y

Livery: White

Aberconwy Borough Council fell below the threshold on fleet size in the 1985 Transport Act and was not required to form a stand-alone company as were all other municipally-owned undertakings. However, change was still forthcoming as, under local government reorganisation, the authority disappeared on 1st April 1996, replaced by the County Borough of Aberconwy and Colwyn, subsequently renamed the County Borough of Conwy. Through all this Great Orme Tours have continued operating and, in a gesture of nostalgia, returned this 1948 Guy Wolf, which was new to Llandudno UDC, to service in 1995. *Ralph Stevens*

Gwynfor Hughes has been operating minibuses in Llangefni since his first Ford Transit purchased from Greater Manchester Fire Service in 1981. The first Mercedes-Benz arrived in 1984 and regular purchases continued until 1990 when F888CRN was acquired after demonstration duties. *John Jones*

GWYN WILLIAMS

Gwyn Williams & Sons Ltd, Derlwyn Garage, Lower Tumble,
Carmarthenshire SA15 5YT

78	BWK8T	Bedford YMT	Plaxton Supreme IV	C53F	1979	Ex Morris Travel, Pencoed, 1981
79	4858DW	Bedford YMT	Duple Dominant II	C53F	1980	Ex Morris Travel, Pencoed, 1981
87	NNM440P	Ford R1114	Plaxton Supreme III	C53F	1976	Ex Radio Coaches, Edmonton, 1984
89	TPC244S	Ford R1114	Plaxton Supreme III	C53F	1978	Ex Pulham, Bourton, 1984
95	SJI2154	Leyland Tiger TRCTL11/2R	Plaxton Viewmaster IV Exp	C49F	1982	Ex Vale of Llangollen, 1986
98	XRJ257S	Ford R1114	Plaxton Supreme III	C53F	1978	Ex Probets, Portishead, 1987
100	5652MT	Leyland Tiger TRCTL11/2R	Plaxton Viewmaster IV Exp	C49F	1982	Ex Vale of Llangollen, 1987
101	E669ECJ	Renault Master T35D	Coachwork Walker	M16	1987	Ex Jenkins, Crickhowell, 1988
102	E333NBX	Renault Master T35D	Williams	M8	1988	
103	F770SBX	Renault Trafic	Williams	M8	1988	Ex van, 1989
104	F550DCY	Freight Rover Sherpa	Freight Rover	M12	1989	
105	SJI2155	Leyland Tiger TRCTL11/3R	Duple 320	C53FT	1986	Ex Watson, Annfield Plain, 1989
106	C83GTH	Renault Trafic	Williams	M8	1986	Ex van, 1989
107	G888HCY	Leyland-DAF 400	Leyland-DAF	M16	1989	
108	G555HTH	Leyland-DAF 200	Leyland-DAF	M12	1989	
109	G500XBX	Renault Trafic	Holdsworth	M8	1989	
110	JIL5231	Renault Master T35D	Williams	M16	1986	Ex van, 1989
111	F242VBX	Renault Trafic	Williams	M8	1989	Ex van, 1989
113	G848VBX	Renault Trafic	Williams	M8	1989	
114	G300LEP	Dennis Javelin 12SDA1907	Duple 320	C53F	1990	
115	JIL5230	Renault Master T35D	Williams	M14	1988	Ex van, 1990
117	H930EBX	Renault Trafic	Williams	M12	1990	
118	H10WMW	Renault Master T35D	Cymric	M12	1991	
120	H650REP	Renault Master T35D	Cymric	M16	1991	
121	H20DBW	Dennis Javelin 12SDA1907	Duple 320	C55FT	1991	
122	SJI2156	Renault Master T35D	Cymric	M16	1989	Ex van, 1991
123	SJI2153	Leyland Leopard PSU3B/4R	Plaxton Elite III	C53F	1973	Ex Tenby Bus & Coach, 1991
124	D387SGS	Freight Rover Sherpa	Dormobile	B16F	1987	Ex Smith, Kennford, 1994
125	B634BEP	Mercedes-Benz L207D	Williams	M8L	1985	Ex van, 1994

Representing the Gwyn Williams coach fleet is GDZ886, a Van Hool-bodied Leyland Tiger with nearside emergency door. *Tony Moyes*

The Gwyn Williams fleet comprises a large number of minibuses, predominantly Renault, that are used on special needs contracts in Carmarthenshire. They are, however, fully liveried in the operators two-tone blue using red signage. Seen in Swansea is an 11 metre Leyland Tiger with a Plaxton Viewmaster Express body, SJI2154. *John Jones*

126	GDZ886	Leyland Tiger TRCTL11/3RZ	Van Hool Alizée	C55F	1985	Ex Merlyns, Skewen, 1994
127	E634YWL	Freight Rover Sherpa	Williams	M8L	1988	Ex van, 1994
128	D946KBU	Renault Master T35D	Cunliffe	M8L	1987	Ex Brecon Dial-a-Ride, 1994
129	D958WJH	Freight Rover Sherpa	Dormobile	B16F	1986	Ex Brian Isaac, Morriston, 1994
130	D147NON	Freight Rover Sherpa	Carlyle	B18F	1987	Ex Phil Anslow, Pontypool, 1994
131	D52MBO	Freight Rover Sherpa	Dormobile	B16F	1986	Ex Phil Anslow, Pontypool, 1994
132	TPL166S	Bedford YMT	Duple Dominant	B53F	1977	Ex Meurig Morgan, Lampeter, 1995
133	H694FFJ	Volkswagen Transporter LT31	Devon Conversions	M12L	1990	Ex Brecon Dial-a-Ride, 1995
134	VCY401	Dennis Dorchester SDA803	Plaxton Paramount 3200	C53F	1983	Ex Thomas Bros, Llangadog, 1995
135						
136	D458CKV	Freight Rover Sherpa	Rootes	B16F	1986	Ex G & G, 1995
	YDR224	DAF MB200DKVL600	Jonckheere Jubilee P50	C50FT	1986	Ex Byron's, Skewen, 1996
	N709AOJ	LDV 400	LDV	M16	1996	

Previous Registrations:

4858DW	ENY26V	SJI2154	GCA122X, 2378VT, 591DW, LBX948J
5652MT	GCA125X, 467VT, SNT806X	SJI2155	D959VTN, GW133, D959VTN
GDZ886	B328AMH	SJI2156	F726UBX
JIL5230	E26NBX	VCY401	A794LCX
JIL5231	C103HTH	YDR224	C422LRP, HBZ4673, C993VDL
SJI2153	NAE887L, 680XAE, JDF149L, 4183MW, NAE887L		

Livery: Two-tone blue and red

The latest addition to the James Brothers fleet is this Caetano Algarve II-bodied Volvo B10M mark IV. It received the cherished number from its predecessor on first registration which is becoming more common. 6738UN was photographed in March 1996 at Llangeitho. *John Jones*

Duple Caribbean 2-bodied Leyland Tiger, D372UVL, was added to the James Brothers fleet in 1995. This provides an interesting contrast with the more modern Volvo shown above. *John Jones*

JAMES BROTHERS

T M G & D E James, Glanyrafon Garage, Llangeitho, Tregaron, Cardiganshire, SY25 6TJ

Depots : Glanyrafon Garage, Llangeltho and Heulfryn, Bronant

LTR997R	Bedford YMT	Plaxton Supreme III	DP53F	1976	Ex Ffoshelig Motors, 1984
SFF756T	Bedford YLQ	Plaxton Supreme IV Express	C45F	1979	Ex D James, Llangeitho, 1980
AUJ746T	Bedford YLQ	Duple Dominant II	C45F	1979	Ex Evans, Tregaron, 1992
WLG999W	Bedford YLQ	Plaxton Supreme IV	C35F	1980	Ex Hanmer, Wrexham. 1983
PNA963W	Bedford YMQ	Duple Dominant II	C45F	1981	Ex Evans, Tregaron, 1992
GVJ522X	Bedford YLQ	Plaxton Supreme IV Express	C45F	1981	
CFF25Y	Leyland Leopard PSU3F/5R	Duple Dominant IV	C49F	1982	
A44KLF	Mercedes-Benz L307D	Reeve Burgess	M12	1984	Ex M & M, Harrow Weald, 1985
C745TJF	Bedford YNT	Plaxton Paramount 3500 II	C53F	1985	
D372UVL	Leyland Tiger TRCTL11/3R	Duple Caribbean 2	C49FT	1986	Ex Hedon Silverwing, Hull, 1995
E753JAY	Dennis Javelin 11SDA1905	Duple 320	C53F	1988	
E330OMG	Mercedes-Benz 609D	Reeve Burgess Beaver	B20F	1988	Ex Arrow, Bristol, 1993
F426ENB	Mercedes-Benz 609D	Made-to-Measure	C23F	1988	Ex Cunningham, Stanford, 1989
F602HEC	Dennis Javelin 11SDL1906	Duple 320	C53F	1988	Ex Browns, Ambleside, 1994
F21TMP	Mercedes-Benz 709D	Reeve Burgess Beaver	B25F	1989	Ex Jim Stones, Glazebury, 1991
329UWL	Dennis Javelin 8.5SDA1926	Plaxton Paramount 3200 III	C35F	1992	
164EWN	Toyota Coaster HZB50R	Caetano Optimo III	C21F	1994	
6738UN	Volvo B10M-62	Caetano Algarve II	C49FT	1995	

Previous Registrations:

164EWN	From new	329UWL	From new	6738UN	From new

Livery: Red and white; red, white and gold (most coaches)

James Brothers operate nine services though these are mostly operated on selected days each week. Service 588 from Pontrhydfendigaid to Lampeter through Tregaron runs four days per week and is thus their prime service. It is generally operated by either F21TMP, seen here outside the depot in Llangeitho, or E330OMG. *John Jones*

JOHN'S TRAVEL

J F H Ithell, 1 Bryn Maelor, Southsea, Wrexham LL11 6RD

UFM999V	Bedford CFL	Steedrive Parflo	M12	1980	Ex Star Mini, Wrexham, 1982
BFP248Y	Mercedes-Benz L307D	Reeve Burgess	M12	1983	Ex A&J, Wrexham, 1992
D103UJC	Freight Rover Sherpa	Dormobile	B16F	1986	Ex Crosville Cymru, 1991

Livery: White & red

JONES INTERNATIONAL

M & M Jones, Bron-y-de, Gwynfe Road, Ffairfach, Llandeilo, Carmarthenshire SA19 6UY

Depot : Station Road, Llandeilo

BCJ710B	Leyland Tiger Cub PSUC1/12T	Harrington Grenadier	C45F	1964	Ex Martin Perry, Bromyard, 1992
BXI637	Leyland Tiger TRCTL11/3R	Plaxton Paramount 3500	C49FT	1983	Ex Procter, Fenton, 1988
B10MMJ	Volvo B10M-61	Van Hool Alizée	C49FT	1984	Ex Lewis, Whitland, 1993
730MMJ	DAF MB230LB615	Van Hool Alizée	C51FT	1988	Ex Welsh's, Upton, 1990

Previous Registrations:

730MMJ	E323EVH	B10MMJ	B238VBH, HIL4424	BXI637	DVT994Y

Livery: Yellow and blue

Jones International are regular contractors to National Express although no vehicles are operated in their corporate colours. To cover busy periods this small fleet is supplemented by short period hires. Leyland Tiger BXI637, while being the oldest front-line coach, remains in immaculate condition. It was photographed when in Cardiff for a rugby international.
John Jones

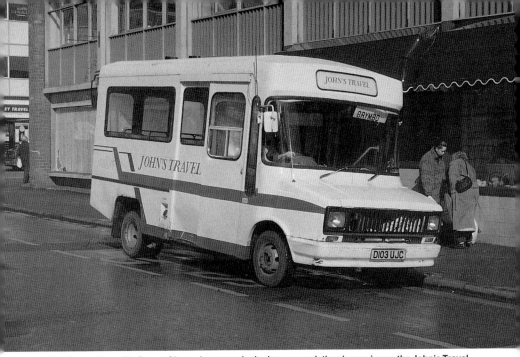

This former Crosville Cymru Sherpa has now clocked up as much time in service on the John's Travel route from Wrexham to Brymbo as it had spent with its former owner. D103UJC is seen at its regular terminus adjacent to Wrexham bus station which is to be extensively re-developed. *John Jones*

Jones International retains this Harrington Grenadier-bodied Leyland Tiger Cub as a full PCV and it is often found on service, especially school contracts. It was new to Wye Valley Motors some ten years before the business was sold to Yeomans. *Byron Gage*

JONES LLANFAETHLU

O R Jones & Sons Ltd, The Bus & Coach Depot, Llanfaethlu, Anglesey LL65 4NW

ECT912	Bedford OB	Duple Vista	C29F	1950	Ex Stevensons, Spath, 1992
CNP316B	Bedford J2SZ10	Plaxton Consort	C20F	1964	Ex Nippy, Sutton, 1980
WWY905L	Bedford YRT	Plaxton Elite III Express	DP53F	1973	Ex West Yorkshire PTE, 1981
u/r	Leyland National 1151/2R		B D	1974	Ex Manchester Airport, 1995
GFJ662N	Leyland National 1151/2R		B D	1974	Ex R Bullock, Cheadle, 1995
JDT436N	Leyland National 10351/2R		B40F	1975	Ex Orion, Kirkcaldy, 1993
BVU917N	Leyland National 10351/1R		B41F	1978	Ex CMT, Aintree, 1995
JWG193P	Leyland National 10351/2R		B40D	1975	Ex Orion, Kirkcaldy, 1993
KSO74P	Leyland National 10351/2R		B40D	1976	Ex Orion, Kirkcaldy, 1993
JTH780P	Leyland National 11351A/1R		B52F	1976	Ex South Wales, 1991
JTH785P	Leyland National 11351A/1R		B52F	1976	Ex South Wales, 1991
NPK235R	Leyland National 10351A/1R		B41F	1976	Ex London Country NW, 1990
TUP329R	Bristol VRT/SL3/501	Eastern Coach Works	H43/31F	1976	Ex Go-Ahead Northern, 1991
PPE658R	Bedford YMT	Duple Dominant II	C53F	1977	Ex Mountford, Harpurhey, 1989
RDC106R	Bristol VRT/SL3/6LXB	Northern Counties	H43/31F	1977	Ex Cleveland Transit, 1990
RDC113R	Bristol VRT/SL3/6LXB	Northern Counties	H43/31F	1977	Ex Cleveland Transit, 1990
RDC114R	Bristol VRT/SL3/6LXB	Northern Counties	H43/31F	1977	Ex Cleveland Transit, 1990
USE633R	Bedford YMT	Duple Dominant	C49F	1977	Ex Short, Glenrothes, 1990
KGD54T	Volvo B58-61	Plaxton Supreme IV	C53F	1979	Ex Leon's, Stafford, 1987
JBR692T	Leyland National 11351A/1R		B49F	1978	Ex Clarkson, South Elmsall, 1995
A345VEP	DAF MB200DKFL600	Plaxton Paramount 3500	C51FT	1983	Ex McCormick, Airdrie, 1993
AEY365	Bova FHD12.280	Bova Futura	C49FT	1984	Ex Boulton, Cardington, 1987
A7ORJ	Bova FHD12.280	Bova Futura	C45FT	1985	Ex Crosville Cymru, 1990
AEY220	Bova FHD12.280	Bova Futura	C53F	1986	Ex South Yorkshire, 1995
D810KWT	Freight Rover Sherpa	Dormobile	B16F	1987	Ex West Riding, 1990
D166VRP	Mercedes-Benz L608D	Alexander AM	B20F	1986	Ex Crosville Cymru, 1995
D955UDY	Mercedes-Benz L608D	Reeve Burgess	B20F	1986	Ex Crosville Cymru, 1995
F947CUA	Freight Rover Sherpa	Carlyle	B18F	1988	Ex Yorkshire Rider, 1993
H964LEY	Mercedes-Benz 709D	Reeve Burgess Beaver	B25F	1990	
H9CCH	Toyota Coaster HBD30R	Caetano Optimo II	C18F	1991	Ex Cross Country Hire, Staplehill, 1994

Previous Registrations:

A7ORJ	B58DMB	BVU917N	JNA584N, 168WAL	JWG193P	JWG193P, 2443MAN
AEY220	C23EUG	ECT912	From new	KGD54T	SDR439T, OTG551
AEY365	9569KM,A400KAY	JDT436N	JDT436N, 3812MAN	KSO74P	KSO74P, 4294MAN

Livery: White, red and green; white and blue (B&I Line)

Jones Llanfaethlu's four double-deckers are all Bristol VRTs though only TUP329R, seen here, has Eastern Coach Works bodywork.
Paul Wigan

Jones Llanfaethlu are currently contracted by Irish Ferries to provide passenger transport within the Port of Holyhead and on the ferry to Dublin. All Leyland Nationals in the fleet, plus Bristol WWY905L, do not see service on public roads and therefore operate on Class V licences. JWG193P is seen in Dublin. *Paul Wigan*

Until 1995 Jones Llanfaethlu operated Bws Gwynedd service 36 from Llangefni to Pencraig but this has now passed to Ellis on re-tendering. Mercedes-Benz H964LEY, seen here in Llangefni before the changes, could now be found on one of Jones' other services from Holyhead to South Stack, Rhoscolyn or Rhosneigr as well as the twice-weekly Llanrhuddlad to Llangefni journeys. *Brian West*

Jones have purchased Dennis Javelins since 1989 when *(above)* **G744YDE**, a shorter version with Plaxton Paramount 3200 bodywork arrived to replace a 1983 Bedford. Unusually, the business was then appointed Dennis agents for the area and their extensive and modern premises play host to other operators vehicles for servicing. Two pairs of full-size Javelins have arrived since and these Plaxton Premiéres operate with 57 seats. Jones was the first Welsh operator of the new Premiére range when a Volvo arrived in 1992. This carried a new livery from which some features have been retained on subsequent purchases as shown *(below)* by **N390KDE**. *John Jones/Vernon Morgan*

JONES of LOGIN

Jones Motors (Login) Ltd, Isfryn, Login, Clunderwen, Carmarthenshire   SA34 0UX

PJF908R	Bedford YLQ	Caetano Cascais II	C45F	1976	Ex Devonways, Totnes, 1986
UDE351T	Bedford YMT	Plaxton Supreme IV Express	C53F	1979	Ex Pioneer, Laugharne, 1980
XBX467T	Bedford YMT	Plaxton Supreme IV Express	C53F	1979	
BDE792V	Bedford YMT	Plaxton Supreme IV	C53F	1980	
GBX484W	Bedford YNT	Duple Dominant IV	C53F	1981	
JUH229W	Leyland Leopard PSU4F/2R	Duple Dominant	B47F	1981	Ex Merthyr Tydfil, 1989
JUH230W	Leyland Leopard PSU4F/2R	Duple Dominant	B47F	1981	Ex Merthyr Tydfil, 1989
HBX972X	Bedford YMT	Duple Dominant	B53F	1981	
GDE148X	Volvo B58-56	Plaxton Supreme VI	C53F	1982	Ex Kerricabs, Newport, 1985
YDE679	Volvo B10M-61	Plaxton Paramount 3500	C53F	1984	
963CDE	Volvo B10M-61	Duple 340	C53FT	1987	
526FDE	Volvo B10M-61	Duple 340	C53FT	1988	
G744YDE	Dennis Javelin 8.5SDA1915	Plaxton Paramount 3200 III	C31FT	1989	
834TDE	Volvo B10M-60	Plaxton Paramount 3500 III	C50F	1991	Ex Wallace Arnold, 1994
521WDE	Volvo B10M-60	Plaxton Paramount 3500 III	C50F	1991	Ex Wallace Arnold, 1994
J918ODE	Volvo B10M-60	Plaxton Premiere 350	C49FT	1992	
K647RDE	Leyland-DAF 400	Crystals	B12F	1992	
K648RDE	Leyland-DAF 400	Crystals	B12F	1992	
K649RDE	Leyland-DAF 400	Crystals	B16F	1992	
K650RDE	Leyland-DAF 400	Crystals	C16F	1992	
L975VDE	Leyland-DAF 400	Autobus Classique	C16F	1994	
M370CDE	Toyota Coaster HZB50R	Caetano Optimo III	C21F	1994	
M589CDE	LDV 400 LDV	M8		1994	
M459DDE	Dennis Javelin 12SDA2131	Plaxton Premiére 320	C53F	1995	
M460DDE	Dennis Javelin 12SDA2131	Plaxton Premiére 320	C53F	1995	
N389KDE	Dennis Javelin 12SDA2155	Plaxton Premiére 320	C57F	1996	
N390KDE	Dennis Javelin 12SDA2155	Plaxton Premiére 320	C57F	1996	

Previous Registrations:

521WDE	H604UWR	834TDE	H603UWR	GDE148X	NKG98X, 521WDE
526FDE	E239NDE	963CDE	D963HDE	YDE679	A475TBX

Livery: Turquoise, white and blue

Second-hand purchases are relatively rare for Jones of Login but this Plaxton Supreme VI-bodied Volvo was acquired when quite young and, even then, it had an earlier operator. A period with a cherished index mark has meant that it now carries a local mark.
John Jones

E JONES & SONS PASSENGER

D & G Jones, Clydfan, Hall Street, Rhosllanerchrugog, Wrexham, LL14 2LG

Depot :Acrefair

FBX561W	Bedford YMQ	Duple Dominant	B50F	1981	Ex Davis Bros, Pencader, 1986
TTA650X	Dennis Lancet SD502	Wadham Stringer Vanguard	B52F	1981	Ex Tillingbourne Valley, 1988
MEP970X	Dennis Lancet SD508	Wadham Stringer Vanguard	B53F	1982	Ex Bowers, Bridgend, 1991
E98DMA	Leyland Tiger TRCTL11/3R	Plaxton Derwent	DP52F	1987	Ex MoD, 1996
K367TJF	Mercedes-Benz 811D	Dormobile Routemaker	B33F	1992	Ex Whitehead, Smithybridge, 1995

Previous Registrations:

E98DMA   87KF16

Livery: Blue and white

The interesting title used by this operator is to enable two former partners in E Jones & Son to operate separately from other members of the family. It was originally expected that this operation would concentrate on bus operation. Showing the slight livery changes to this fleet is Dennis Lancet, **TTA650X**. *John Jones*

E JONES & SONS

JB & G Jones, Mountain View, Bank Street, Ponciau, Wrexham LL14 1EN

WTL949S	Bedford YLQ	Plaxton Supreme III Express	C45F	1977	Ex Holloway, Scunthorpe, 1982
BBM62A	Volvo B58-61	Plaxton Viewmaster IV	C44FT	1980	Ex Sampson, Cheshunt, 1990
HSC175X	Leyland Cub CU435	Duple Dominant	B31F	1981	Ex Lothian, 1991
YJO957X	Volvo B10M-61	Plaxton Viewmaster IV	C51F	1982	Ex Motts, Stoke Mandeville, 1994
N7EJS	Dennis Dart 9.8SDL30	Plaxton Pointer	B40F	1995	

Previous Registrations:

BBM62A	KAY10V	YJO957X	YBW473X, 5812MT

Livery: Blue, white and orange

The portion of E Jones & Son to retain that name originally concentrated on private hire and contracts. In the summer of 1995 a contract with the local authority was awarded for the former Crosville Cymru service from Garden Village to Borras. For this work a new Dennis Dart, N7EJS, has been placed in service and is seen during April 1996. A Leyland Cub provides cover when needed. *Tom Johnson*

W E JONES & SON

G E Jones, The Garage, Llanerchymedd, Anglesey LL71 8EB

Depots :Brynteg Farm, Benllech and The Garage, Llanerchymedd

OCR162G	Leyland Atlantean PDR1/1	East Lancashire	H45/31F	1968	Ex Weller, Midhurst, 1989
SEL247H	Leyland Atlantean PDR1A/1	Alexander J	H43/31F	1969	Ex Lancaster, 1989
OVK144M	Leyland Atlantean AN68/1R	Alexander AL	H43/34F	1973	Ex Woolley, Llanedwen, 1993
NSG216M	Bedford YRT	Duple Dominant Express	C53F	1973	Ex Carreglefn Coaches, 1995
SMU919N	Daimler Fleetline CRL6	Park Royal	H44/27D	1974	Ex Woolley, Llanedwen, 1993
5889VC	Volvo B58-61	Plaxton Supreme III	C48FT	1976	Ex Hall, Newton Aycliffe, 1991
OJV121S	Leyland Fleetline FE30AGR	Roe	H45/29D	1977	Ex East Midland (Grimsby), 1996
WPJ8S	Bedford YMT	Duple Dominant II	C53F	1978	Ex Browne, Smallfield, 1980
AEC732S	Bedford YMT	Plaxton Supreme III	C53F	1978	Ex Woolley, Llanedwen, 1991
DVR301T	Ford R1114	Plaxton Supreme IV	C53F	1979	Ex Woolley, Llanedwen, 1991
A741DCN	Leyland Royal Tiger B50	Roe Doyen	C44FT	1983	Ex Hart Coaches, Hart, 1994
B218JPH	Mercedes-Benz L608D	Coachcraft	C21F	1984	Ex Evans of Pwllheli, 1991

Previous Registrations:

5889VC	NGB7P		
		A741DCN	A213XJR, JCN822

Livery: Red and cream

W E Jones often parks double-deck buses in a lay-by on the road south from Amlwch during the school day to reduce unnecessary travel. Here, veteran Atlantean OCR162G awaits the return of its driver for the home-bound journey. *Brian West*

K D COACH HIRE

A Kerfoot-Davies, Inglewood, Axton, Holywell, Flintshire CH8 9DH

UPC63X	Mercedes-Benz L508D	Reeve Burgess	C19F	1982	Ex Sunbury Coaches, 1993
UHH173X	Leyland Leopard PSU3F/5R	Duple Dominant IV	C53F	1982	Ex Pheonex Travel, Gosport, 1995
D775RBU	Renault-Dodge S56	Northern Counties	B20F	1987	Ex GMS Buses, 1996
D543HNW	Ford Transit	Carlyle	B16F	1986	Ex Ralph Bullock, Cheadle, 1994
F757WSC	Iveco Daily 49.10	Carlyle Dailybus 2	DP25F	1989	Ex Martin, Motherwell, 1994

KD Coach Hire started operating in 1993. Two services are operated on contract to the County Council, these being Pensarn to Abergele hospital and three Denbigh rural journeys. In addition, a service in Rhyl is also provided and Iveco F757WSC is seen operating it. *John Jones*

K M P

KMP (Llanberis) Ltd, Y Glyn, Llanberis, Gwynedd, LL55 4HN.

JWW226N	Bristol VRT/SL2/6G	Eastern Coach Works	H43/31F	1975	Ex York City & District, 1989
HMA564T	Leyland National 10351B/1R		B44F	1978	Ex Jones Llanfaethlu, 1991
JTU596T	Leyland National 10351B/1R		B44F	1979	Ex Midland, 1995
BVR87T	Leyland Fleetline FE30AGR	Northern Counties	H43/32F	1979	Ex Yorkshire Rider, 1995
WTH957T	Bristol VRT/SL3/501	Eastern Coach Works	H43/31F	1979	Ex Brewers, 1993
BEP964V	Bristol VRT/SL3/501	Eastern Coach Works	H43/31F	1979	Ex Brewers, 1993
BEP969V	Bristol VRT/SL3/501	Eastern Coach Works	H43/31F	1980	Ex Brewers, 1994
EDT917V	Bristol VRT/SL3/501	Eastern Coach Works	H43/31F	1980	Ex RoadCar, 1995
E302HHP	Peugot Talbot Pullman	Talbot	DP22F	1988	Ex Peugeot Talbot, 1988
772URB	Volvo B10M-61	Duple 340	C55F	1988	Ex Waddon, Bedwas, 1994
6697RU	Volvo B10M-61	Duple 340	C55F	1988	Ex Waddon, Bedwas, 1994
7CCH	Volvo B10M-60	Plaxton Paramount 3500 III	C49F	1989	Ex Dodsworth, Boroughbridge, 1993
A7KMP	Volvo B10M-60	Plaxton Paramount 3500 III	C49F	1989	Ex Dodsworth, Boroughbridge, 1993
J59NJT	Volvo B10M-60	Plaxton Premiére 350	C49FT	1992	Ex Excelsior, 1996
J117NJT	Volvo B10M-60	Plaxton Premiére 350	C49FT	1992	Ex Excelsior, 1996
L77KMP	Volvo B10M-62	Jonckheere Deauville 65	C51FT	1994	
L777KMP	Volvo B10M-62	Jonckheere Deauville 65	C51FT	1994	
M7KMP	Volvo B10M-62	Jonckheere Deauville 65	C51FT	1994	
M777KMP	Volvo B10M-62	Plaxton Premiére 350	C49FT	1995	
M637BEY	Mercedes-Benz 814D	Mellor	B31F	1995	
N776CJC	Mercedes-Benz 814D	Mellor	B31F	1995	
N77KMP	Volvo B10M-62	Plaxton Premiére 350	C49FT	1996	
N777KMP	Volvo B10M-62	Plaxton Premiére 350	C49FT	1996	

Previous Registrations:

7CCH	F716EUG	772URB	E408RWR
6697RU	E409RWR	A7KMP	F717EUG

Livery: Blue and black; white and red (Bus Eireann) 7CCH, 772URB, 6697RU; Eurolines A7KMP, M7KMP, M777KMP.

Opposite top: **M637BEY is the first of a pair of Mellor bodied Mercedes Benz 814s acquired in 1995 to complement the full-size buses on tendered services. The southern end of the Llyn Padarn is seen in the background as the vehicle approaches Llanberis, one of the popular tourist areas of north Wales.** *Paul Wigan*

Opposite bottom: **While operating a modern coach fleet, KMP also operate local services with a bus fleet that includes two Leyland Nationals and six double-decks, five of which are Bristol VRs. WTH957T is seen at Llanberis, close to the rail station from which steam trains begin the ascent of Snowdon.** *Paul Wigan*

Peugeot Talbot have now supplied several of their Pullman tri-axle minibus and the welfare equivalent, the Freeway. The latter appears more common as it features in many local authority fleets. The PCV version is seen less and one example, E302HHP, has been operated for KMP for eight years. It is seen in Llanberis. *John Jones*

T S LEWIS

T S Lewis, Penrhiwpal Garage, Rhydlewis, Llandyssul, Cardiganshire SA44 5QG

DJH731F	Bedford VAL70	Plaxton Panorama	C52F	1968	Ex Jones, Login, 1972
MIB3230	Bedford YRQ	Plaxton Elite III	C45F	1975	Ex Eynon, Trimsaran, 1978
NIA8450	Bedford YRQ	Duple Dominant	C45F	1975	Ex Gwalia Bus Service, Llanybydder, 1989
779HCY	Bedford YRT	Plaxton Supreme III	C53F	1975	Ex Thompson, Southall, 1976
NIA9778	Bedford YRT	Plaxton Supreme III	C53F	1976	Ex Kinch, Mountsorrel, 1977
NIA8778	Bedford YLQ	Plaxton Supreme III	C45F	1977	Ex Hanmer, Southsea, 1980
VNM239S	Bedford YLQ	Duple Dominant II	C45F	1977	Ex Emlyn Coaches, Capel Iwan, 1995
NIA9896	Leyland Leopard PSU3E/4R	Plaxton Supreme III	C53F	1978	Ex Hanmer, Southsea, 1980
600DBX	Bedford VAS5	Plaxton Supreme III	C29F	1979	Ex Collins, Roch, 1987
600KPU	Bedford YLQ	Plaxton Supreme IV	C45F	1979	Ex Bysiau Cwm Taf, Whitland, 1994
DPB777T	Leyland Leopard PSU3E/4R	Duple Dominant II	C53F	1979	Ex Bicknell, Godalming, 1980
GMB391T	Leyland National 11351A/1R		B49F	1978	Ex Emlyn Coaches, Capel Iwan, 1995
SEJ386	Leyland Tiger TRCTL11/3R	Plaxton Paramount 3500	C50FT	1984	Ex Hodgson, Chatburn, 1987
FIW578	Bedford YNV Venturer	Plaxton Paramount 3200 II	C57F	1985	Ex Hunting Brae, Aldermaston, 1996
108BDL	Leyland Tiger TRCTL11/3RZ	Plaxton Paramount 3500 III	C53F	1987	Ex Hills of Tredegar, 1991
E855FVJ	Bedford CF	Dormobile	M12	1987	Ex Emlyn Coaches, Capel Iwan, 1994
F21YBO	Kässbohrer Setra S215HDI	Kässbohrer Tornado	C49FT	1989	Ex Bebb, Llantwit Fardre, 1991
K4CYM	Renault Trafic	Cymric	M14	1993	Ex Emlyn Coaches, Capel Iwan, 1994

Previous Registrations:

108BDL	D65MWO	FIW578	C510HSE	NIA9778	NJF864P
600DBX	EGS159T	MIB3230	HFP118N	NIA9896	DTU48S
600KPU	UFT926T	NIA8450	JFF342P	SEJ286	A351RCK
779HCY	KVD447P	NIA8778	ACA190S		

Livery: Cream, red and orange

T S Lewis operates from a large garage in the hamlet of Penrhiwpal about seven kilometres from Newcastle Emlyn. During 1995 the business of Emlyn Coaches was acquired including their Leyland National. This bus is not currently in use, but it is expected to be at a later date. Pictured here is 108BDL, seen leaving the depot for an afternoon schools journey. *John Jones*

LEWIS WHITLAND

F E Lewis, The Garage, King Edward Street, Whitland, Carmarthenshire SA34 0AA

OOR320G	Bedford VAL70	Plaxton Panorama II	C52F	1969	Ex Holmes, Cheshunt, 1991
LPJ323P	Bedford YRQ	Duple Dominant	C45F	1976	Ex Bysiau Cwm Taf, Whitland, 1993
MPG153P	Leyland Leopard PSU3C/4R	Duple Dominant	B53F	1976	Ex Ffoshelig Motors, 1996
GMS305S	Leyland Leopard PSU3E/4R	Alexander AYS	B53F	1978	Ex Ffoshelig Motors, 1996
OPL77W	Leyland Leopard PSU3F/5R	Plaxton Supreme IV	C53F	1981	Ex Bicknell, Godalming, 1986
RPC59X	Leyland Leopard PSU3F/5R	Plaxton Supreme IV	C53F	1982	Ex Bicknell, Godalming, 1986
SCD693X	Leyland Leopard PSU3F/5R	Plaxton Supreme V	C53F	1982	Ex Bicknell, Godalming, 1989
NRL687X	Leyland Tiger TRCTL11/2R	Plaxton Supreme V Express	C53F	1982	Ex Evans, Tregaron, 1995
A233GNR	Volvo B10M-61	Duple Dominant IV	C53F	1984	Ex Ffoshelig Motors, 1996
E716BDM	Mercedes-Benz L307D	Advanced Vehicle Bodies	M12	1988	Ex Chartercoach, Great Oakley, 1991
F866TNH	Toyota Coaster HB31R	Caetano Optimo	C21F	1988	Ex Davis, Minchinhampton, 1992
H2WJL	Leyland Tiger TR2R62C21Z5/8	Plaxton Paramount 3500 III	C51FT	1991	
K4DAF	Leyland-DAF 400	Leyland-DAF	M16	1992	Ex Green's demonstrator, 1993

Previous Registrations:
NRL687X   NRL687X, PJI8360

Livery: White, green and gold

Old white house by the (river) Taf' is the literal translation of Hen dy gwyn ar Daf here carried by Leyland Tiger H2WJL. The anglicised version of the town's name is Whitland. Lewis Whitland's smart fleet carries a livery derived from that of Bicknell, Godalming from whom several vehicles have been acquired in the past. *John Jones*

LEWIS Y LLAN

A H & R M Lewis, Madyn Industrial Estate, Amlwch, Anglesey, LL68 9DL

GBD777T	Bedford YMT	Plaxton Supreme IV	C53F	1979	Ex Cresta Cars, Bridgend, 1994
BVJ771V	Ford R1114	Duple Dominant II	C53F	1980	Ex Bennett, Gloucester, 1985
BVJ780V	Bedford YMT	Plaxton Supreme IV Express	C53F	1980	Ex Cresta Cars, Bridgend, 1994
341TJ	Leyland Royal Tiger B50	Roe Doyen	C46FT	1983	Ex Gardiner, Holytown, 1993
UCK277	Volvo B10M-61	Jonckheere Jubilee P50	C51FT	1983	Ex Shaw Hadwin, Silverdale, 1994
H272LJC	Mercedes Benz 811D	Optare StarRider	B33F	1990	
H273LJC	Mercedes Benz 811D	Optare StarRider	B33F	1990	

Previous Registrations:

341TJ	A603KYG, 23PTA, A506RUG	UCK277	A314XHE

Livery: Red

Lewis y Llan operate two daily services, 60 Amlwch - Cemaes circular and 61 Holyhead - Llanfaethlu - Amlwch. The main performers on these are the two Optare StarRiders which have now commenced their second contract period on Bws Gwynedd work since 1990. The last Bristols left the fleet in 1995 after several years of operation. *John Jones*

LLITHFAEN MOTORS

G H Williams, The Garage, Delfryn, Llithfaen, Gwynedd, LL53 6PA

TUJ921J	Bedford YRQ	Willowbrook 001	DP45F	1970	Ex Morris, Llanfyllin, 1980
FBX560W	Bedford YMQ	Duple Dominant	B53F	1981	Ex Davies Bros, Pencader, 1988
CEJ939Y	Bedford VAS5	Duple Dominant II	C29F	1983	Ex Nefyn Coaches, 1992
D509MJA	Iveco Daily 49.10	Robin Hood City Nippy	B21F	1987	Ex Nefyn Coaches, 1994

Livery: Maroon and cream

Little has changed at Llithfaen during the last two years though many changes have occurred close by. However, one minibus has arrived from the GM Buses batch of Iveco Dailys. Pictured here is **FBX560W**, a Bedford YMQ which previously operated with Davies Bros. who sold a sister vehicle to **E. Jones & Son.** *John Jones*

The P&O Lloyd fleet operate well-presented double-deckers in a smart cream and red livery with similarly attired coaches trimmed with gold. Recently, two pairs of double-decks have arrived, one pair from Blue Bus of Derby and two buses from the Grimsby-Cleethorpes operation of East Midland. *(above)* BCS867T, with Northern Counties bodywork, represents the former pair while *(below)* ULS658T has an Eastern Coach Works body. *Ralph Stevens*

Opposite: **Four Leyland Leopards are retained in the P&O Lloyd fleet, three 12-metre PSU5 models and one 11-metre PSU3. This shorter vehicle, new to Eastern Counties as JVF818V, was photographed in Holywell with its current mark, IIL8744.** *John Jones*

P & O LLOYD

F, D, GM & R Lloyd, Rhydwen Garage, Bagillt, Flintshire, CH6 6JB

GOG554N	Daimler Fleetline CRL6(6LXB)	Park Royal	H43/33F	1975	Ex Western Scottish, 1991
GOG575N	Daimler Fleetline CRL6(6LXB)	Park Royal	H43/33F	1975	Ex Western Scottish, 1991
KON302P	Leyland Fleetline FE30ALR(6LXB)	MCW	H43/33F	1976	Ex West Midlands Travel, 1989
KON358P	Leyland Fleetline FE30ALR	MCW	H43/33F	1976	Ex West Midlands Travel, 1989
OKW519R	Leyland Fleetline FE30AGR	MCW	H46/27F	1977	Ex Farmer, Ashford, 1993
OKW525R	Leyland Fleetline FE30AGR	MCW	H46/31F	1977	Ex Grey Green, Stamford Hill, 1993
SDA637S	Leyland Fleetline FE30AGR	Park Royal	H43/33F	1977	Ex West Midlands Travel, 1989
IIL6252	Leyland Leopard PSU5C/4R	Plaxton Supreme IV	C55F	1978	Ex Epsom Coaches, 1986
WDA679T	Leyland Fleetline FE30AGR	Park Royal	H43/33F	1979	Ex West Midlands Travel, 1989
KFM191T	Leyland Fleetline FE30AGR	Northern Counties	H43/29F	1979	Ex Chester, 1993
ULS658T	Leyland Fleetline FE30AGR	Eastern Coach Works	H43/32F	1979	Ex Western Scottish, 1992
BCS867T	Leyland Fleetline FE30AGR	Northern Counties	H44/31F	1979	Ex Blue Bus, Derby, 1995
IIL8744	Leyland Leopard PSU3E/4R	Plaxton Supreme IV Express	C49F	1979	Ex Goodwin, Stockport, 1992
POI2062	Leyland Leopard PSU5C/4R	Plaxton Supreme IV	C57F	1979	Ex Epsom Coaches, 1986
GTO300V	Leyland Fleetline FE30AGR	Northern Counties	H43/30F	1980	Ex Blue Bus, Derby, 1995
WFU468V	Leyland Fleetline FE30AGR	Roe	H45/31F	1980	Ex East Midland (Grimsby), 1996
XFU128V	Leyland Fleetline FE30AGR	Roe	H45/31F	1980	Ex East Midland (Grimsby), 1996
JIL4404	Leyland Leopard PSU5D/4R	Plaxton Supreme V	C53F	1981	Ex Bodman, Worton, 1994
6709PO	Volvo B10M-61	Duple Caribbean 2	C51F	1984	
POI6312	Volvo B10M-61	Plaxton Paramount 3200 II	C53F	1985	Ex Frames Rickards, Brentford, 1992
5182PO	Volvo B10M-61	Plaxton Paramount 3500 III	C49FT	1988	Ex Wrays, Harrogate, 1994
5373PO	Volvo B10M-61	Plaxton Paramount 3500 III	C51F	1988	Ex Dunn-Line, Nottingham, 1994
F951CUA	Freight Rover Sherpa	Carlyle Citybus 2	B18F	1988	Ex Yorkshire Rider, 1993
J291RNE	Mercedes-Benz 609D	Made-to-Measure	B28F	1992	Ex Llynfi Coaches, Maesteg, 1995

Previous Registrations:

5182PO	E28TYG	IIL8744	JVF818V
5373PO	E241BMA, A4BOB, E358ERR	POI2062	GGT334T
6709PO	B782AMA	POI6312	B530BML
IIL6252	FGJ308T		

Livery: Cream and red; cream, red and gold (coaches)

Longs are based at Abercraf situated in the Swansea Valley above Ystradgynlais. The area is in Powys but close to the borders of Carmarthenshire and the two new unitary authorities of Neath & Port Talbot and Swansea. In 1995 much of the business of D&N Travel was taken on, Freight Rover Sherpas now doing much of the work. G35HDW is seen in Cardiff. *John Jones*

M&H Travel's routes 14, Mold to Denbigh, and 40, Rhyl to Tremeirchion are generally operated by coaches of which JBH390V is typical. Note also the use of the Vale of Clwyd name. *John Jones*

LONGS

DG Long & A J Evans, Rheolau Garage, 3 Heol Rheolau, Abercraf, Powys SA9 1TB

KCY187P	Ford R1114	Plaxton Supreme III	C53F	1975	Ex Joseph Jones & Son, Ystradgynlais, 1990
AKW965T	Bedford YLQ	Duple Dominant II	C45F	1979	Ex Joseph Jones & Son, Ystradgynlais, 1990
YTH930T	Leyland Leopard PSU3E/4R	Plaxton Supreme IV	C53F	1979	Ex Joseph Jones & Son, Ystradgynlais, 1990
ABN772V	Ford R1114	Plaxton Supreme IV	C53F	1975	Ex Durbin, Almondsbury, 1992
BEU809V	Leyland Leopard PSU5C/4R	Plaxton Supreme IV	C53F	1980	Ex Eagle Coaches, Bristol, 1994
ADN51V	Ford R1114	Plaxton Supreme IV	C53F	1975	Ex Eddie Brown, Helperby, 1984
HFX401V	Ford R1114	Plaxton Supreme IV	C53F	1975	Ex James, Burry Port, 1984
LBU630V	Ford R1114	Duple Dominant II	C53F	1980	Ex D&N Travel, Ystradgynlais, 1995
OIB1083	Leyland Leopard PSU5C/4R	Plaxton Supreme V	C48F	1981	Ex Venture Travel, Cardiff, 1994
PNB787W	Ford R1114	Plaxton Supreme IV	C53F	1981	Ex Smiths Shearings, 1986
PNB789W	Ford R1114	Plaxton Supreme IV	C53F	1981	Ex Smiths Shearings, 1986
PNW329W	Ford R1114	Plaxton Supreme IV	C53F	1981	Ex Joseph Jones & Son, Ystradgynlais, 1990
PMO414X	Fiat 60.10	Caetano Beja	C18F	1981	Ex Kestrel Mini Coaches, Luton, 1992
GIL2987	Leyland Tiger TRCTL11/3R	Plaxton Paramount 3500 II	C53F	1985	Ex Vale of Llangollen, 1993
GIL4527	Leyland Tiger TRCTL11/3RZ	Van Hool Alizée	C53F	1986	Ex Shearings, 1992
GIL4128	Leyland Tiger TRCTL11/3RZ	Plaxton Paramount 3500 II	C53F	1986	Ex Vale of Llangollen, 1993
D163NCY	Iveco 60.10	Robin Hood	C19FL	1987	Ex West Glamorgan CC, 1991
D141NON	Freight Rover Sherpa	Carlyle	B18F	1987	Ex Eagle Coaches, Bristol, 1994
D243OOJ	Freight Rover Sherpa	Carlyle	B18F	1987	Ex D&N Travel, Ystradgynlais, 1995
E932RWR	Freight Rover Sherpa	Carlyle Citybus 2	B18F	1987	Ex East Midland, 1996
E348UOH	Freight Rover Sherpa	Carlyle Citybus 2	B21F	1988	Ex D&N Travel, Ystradgynlais, 1995
F480SBX	Renault Trafic	Cymric	M10	1988	Ex van, 1992
G219EOA	Freight Rover Sherpa	Carlyle Citybus 2	B20F	1989	Ex Travel de Courcey, Coventry, 1995
G35HDW	Freight Rover Sherpa	Carlyle Citybus 2	B20F	1990	Ex Travel de Courcey, Coventry, 1995
J986UCY	Ford Transit VE6	Cymric	M14	1991	Ex Days Hire, Swansea, 1994
J189BWJ	Ford Transit VE6	Advanced Vehicle Bodies	M14	1992	Ex Days Hire, Swansea, 1995

Previous Registrations:

BEU809V	BEU809V, 945HU	LBU630V	XRN623V, 711BHR, BRN817V, WUN690
GIL2987	B387DMB, 3810VT, B434FFM	OIB1083	MRJ278W
GIL4128	C711LMA, 8177VT, C738NCA, 467VT	PMO414X	TNR794X, 8896RH
GIL4527	C339DND		

Livery: Cream, yellow & maroon

M & H TRAVEL

M & H H Owen, 8 Tre Wen, Denbigh, Denbighshire LL16 3HF

Depot :Trefnant Garage, Trefnant

AAZ9091	Bedford YRT	Duple Dominant	C53F	1976	Ex Moss, Sandown, 1993
JBH390V	Ford R1114	Duple Dominant II	C53F	1979	Ex AN Andrew, Mostyn, 1992
ACA666A	Bedford YMT	Plaxton Supreme IV	C53F	1979	Ex Strafford's, Cs, Coedpoeth, 1995
WRF833X	Ford R1114	Duple Dominant IV	C53F	1982	Ex Staffordian, Stafford, 1989
FBZ1473	Volvo B10M-61	Duple Goldliner IV	C53F	1982	Ex Safford, Little Gransden, 1993
RJI4378	Volvo B10M-61	Duple Goldliner IV	C50F	1982	Ex Caelloi, Pwllheli, 1992
151WYB	Volvo B10M-61	Plaxton Paramount 3500	C48FT	1983	Ex Caelloi, Pwllheli, 1992
HIL5659	Volvo B10M-61	Plaxton Paramount 3500 III	C53F	1987	Ex Dodsworth, Boroughbridge, 1996
F258DKG	Freight Rover Sherpa (Isuzu)	Carlyle Citybus 2	B20F	1989	Ex Boomerang Bus Co, Tewkesbury, 1996
G216EOA	Freight Rover Sherpa	Carlyle Citybus 2	B20F	1989	Ex West London, Tylers Green, 1996

Previous Registrations:

151WYB	RME974Y	HIL5659	E563UHS
AAZ9091	LDL728P	RJI4378	RSJ812Y
ACA666A	JDM424T, RDM378	SJI2767	D137NON
FBZ1473	FHS744X		

Livery: Yellow, blue and black

MEYERS

M L Meyers, Cilgwyn, Llanpumsaint, Carmarthenshire SA33 6LA

HDF700L	Leyland Leopard PSU3B/4R	Plaxton Elite III	C53F	1973	Ex Pulhams, Bourton, 1993
ATH180T	DAF MB200DKL500	Plaxton Supreme IV	C49F	1979	Ex Evans, Tregaron, 1995
E178TWO	Freight Rover Sherpa	Carlyle Citybus 2	B20F	1988	Ex Hudson, Downley, 1994
F427AWD	Iveco Daily 49.10	Carlyle Dailybus 2	DP25F	1988	Ex Red Rose, Aylesbury, 1994
F481WFA	MCW MetroRider MF154/10	MCW	C29F	1989	Ex Dereham Coachways, 1995

Previous Registrations:

ATH180T	FTW130T, 275NAE	F481WFA	F115UEH, 565LON

Livery: Blue and white; blue and silver

Opposite top: **The integral MetroRider is still proving to be one of the most popular minibuses as the MCW and latterly the Optare product are moving onto the second hand market. Shown here is one of the older MCW examples, F481WFA which is one fitted with high back seating for coach work. It is seen in Cardiff in February 1996.** *John Jones*

Opposite bottom: **While not a major fleet in terms of numbers, the Meyers fleet contains several interesting coaches. HDF700L is a Plaxton bodied Leyland Leopard now some twenty years old though still looking resplendant. The previous owner, Pulhams of Bourton-on-the-Water, is also well known for maintaining coaches in excellent condition.** *John Jones*

Below: **Malcolm Meyers has operated from Llanpumsaint to Carmarthen for several years expanding since successfully gaining Dyfed tendered services in Autumn 1994. These include routes based on Newcastle Emlyn, formerly operated by Emlyn Coaches. Seen departing from Carmarthen is former National Welsh Sherpa E178TWO.** *David Donati*

MID WALES MOTORWAYS

Mid Wales Motorways Ltd, Bwthyn, Penrhyncoch, Aberystwyth,
Cardiganshire SY23 3EH

Depots: Brynhyfryd Garage, Penrhyncoch and Pool Road, Newtown, Powys

NCD551M	Bristol VRT/SL/6LX	Eastern Coach Works	H43/31F	1973	Ex Brighton & Hove, 1988
KCX945N	Bedford YLQ	Duple Dominant	C45F	1975	Ex Clun Valley, Newcastle, 1988
PFF317S	Bedford YMT	Duple Dominant	C53F	1978	Ex Evans, Penrhyncoch, 1991
XEW964T	Bedford YMT	Plaxton Supreme IV	C53F	1979	Ex Dew, Somersham, 1980
LVS434V	Bedford YMT	Plaxton Supreme IV	C53F	1980	Ex Evans, Tregaron, 1995
CGA199X	Volvo B58-61	Van Hool Alizée	C49FT	1982	Ex Darragh, Kilrea, 1988
MAX334X	Leyland Tiger TRCTL11/2R	Plaxton Supreme VI	C53F	1982	Ex Evans, Penrhyncoch, 1991
B590HEJ	Ford Transit 150	Dixon Lomas	M12	1984	Ex Evans, Penrhyncoch, 1991
D113XVX	Ford Transit VE6	Ford	M12	1986	Ex Evans, Penrhyncoch, 1991
E605XWB	Freight Rover Sherpa	Greenhous	M16	1987	Ex Evans, Penrhyncoch, 1991
E728DSO	Toyota Coaster HB31R	Caetano Optimo	C18F	1988	Ex R&I Tours, Park Royal, 1994
G990FVV	LAG G355Z	LAG Panoramic	C49FT	1989	Ex Merlyns, Skewen, 1994
G464VPG	Mercedes-Benz 709D	Reeve Burgess Beaver	B25F	1990	Ex Eurotravel, Woking, 1995
H178EJU	Leyland Tiger TRCL10/3ARZA	Plaxton Paramount 3500 III	C51FT	1990	Ex Evans, Penrhyncoch, 1991
H179EJU	Leyland Tiger TRCL10/3ARZA	Plaxton Paramount 3500 III	C51FT	1990	Ex Evans, Penrhyncoch, 1991
M874UEJ	Volvo B10M-62	Jonckheere Deauville 45	C51FT	1994	
M875UEJ	Volvo B10M-62	Jonckheere Deauville 45	C51FT	1994	

Previous Registrations:
CGA199X   CGA199X, ADZ9525

Livery: White (or cream), blue and yellow; white (Eurolines) M874/5UEJ, H178EJU

Series 1 Bristol VR NCD551M has almost achieved the status of longest serving vehicle in the Mid Wales fleet. Certainly this well-preserved vehicle is the oldest and is now based at Penrhyncoch. It was from Newtown to this village outside Aberystwyth that the bulk of the business moved in 1991 although a handful of vehicles still operate from there. *John Jones*

MIDWAY MOTORS

D W & W S Rees, Midway Garage, Crymych,
Pembrokeshire, SA41 3QU

EDE38R	Ford R1014	Plaxton Supreme III	C45F	1977	Ex Wright, Wrexham, 1980
TEX118R	Ford R1014	Plaxton Supreme III	C45F	1977	Ex Frenni Coaches, Boncath, 1993
NGL371	Ford R1114	Plaxton Supreme III	C53F	1977	Ex Moss, Sandown, 1991
RDL671S	Ford R1014	Duple Dominant	B46F	1977	Ex Isle of Wight CC, 1991
SDL967S	Ford R1014	Duple Dominant	B47F	1978	Ex Isle of Wight CC, 1991
FFP200V	Ford R1114	Duple Dominant II Express	C53F	1979	Ex Ffoshelig Motors, Newchurch, 1994
2934MM	Volvo B10M-61	Jonckheere Bermuda	C48FT	1981	Ex Down, Mary Tavy, 1985
1885FM	Ford R1114	Duple Dominant IV	C53F	1981	Ex Fraser, Accrington, 1986
250DBX	Mercedes-Benz L508D	Devon Conversions	DP24F	1981	Ex Gloucestershire CC, 1993
XNK200X	Ford R1014	Plaxton Bustler	B47F	1981	Ex Universitybus, Hatfield, 1993
LDE578Y	Ford R1114	Plaxton Supreme VI Express	C53F	1982	
WWB323Y	Ford R1114	Plaxton Paramount 3200	C48FT	1983	Ex KM, Lundwood, 1986
GIL3276	Volvo B10M-61	Caetano Algarve	C51F	1984	Ex Byron's, Skewen, 1994
YTH317	Volvo B10M-61	Plaxton Paramount 3500 II	C48FT	1986	Ex Denison, Otley, 1989
D920PGB	Mercedes-Benz 609D	Devon Conversions	C25F	1986	Ex Mason, Bo'ness, 1988
E442YAO	Ford Transit VE6	Mellor	M15	1987	Ex Streamline, Bath, 1993
F207EFK	Ford Transit VE6	Ford	M14	1989	Ex private owner, 1990

Previous Registrations:

1885FM	JFV295W	GIL3276	B252CUH
250DBX	JEU803X	NGL371	ODL774R
2934MM	XNV153W, 645COD, PPF286W	WWB323Y	UWG605Y, 4465KM
EDE38R	VMA410R, 250DBX	YTH317	C453CWR

Livery: Blue and white

The former Isle of Wight Fords are regularly seen on Midway's Monday to Saturday service from Hermon/Crymych to Cardigan. SDL967S passes Finch Square, Cardigan on a return journey.
John Jones

NEFYN COACHES

R G Owen, Gerafon, Nefyn, Gwynedd, LL53 6HE

WWP834V	Bedford YMT	Plaxton Supreme IV	C53F	1980	Ex Evans, Tregaron, 1989
875EPX	Volvo B58-56	Plaxton Supreme IV	C53F	1980	Ex Evans, Tregaron, 1989
SYJ961X	Bedford YMQ	Plaxton Supreme V	C45F	1981	Ex Evans, Tregaron, 1988
A829JEY	Volvo B10M-61	Plaxton Paramount 3200	C50F	1983	Ex Caelloi, Pwllheli, 1992
B258AMG	Bedford YMP	Plaxton Paramount 3200	C45F	1984	Ex Sanders, Holt, 1995
B89CDS	Bedford YNT	Duple Laser 2	C53F	1985	Ex Evans, Tregaron, 1994
D659WEY	Bedford YNT	Plaxton Paramount 3200 II	C53F	1986	Ex Evans, Tregaron, 1994
D143HML	Bedford YNT	Plaxton Paramount 3200 II	C53F	1987	Ex Evans, Tregaron, 1994
A2NPT	Bedford YNV	Duple Laser 2	C53F	1987	Ex Evans, Tregaron, 1995
D40OTH	Mercedes-Benz 609D	PMT	C26F	1987	Ex Evans, Tregaron, 1994
E316ACC	Mercedes Benz 709D	Reeve Burgess Beaver	B25F	1988	
H482SWE	Mercedes Benz 609D	Coachcraft	C21F	1990	Ex Evans, Tregaron, 1995
H838NOC	Iveco Daily 40.8	Carlyle Dailybus 2	B21F	1991	Ex Caelloi, Pwllheli, 1996
H533MCC	Leyland Swift LBM6T/2RS	Reeve Burgess Harrier	B41F	1991	
H741TWB	Mercedes-Benz 709D	Reeve Burgess Beaver	C23F	1991	Ex Patterson's, Birmingham, 1995
H742TWB	Mercedes-Benz 709D	Reeve Burgess Beaver	C23F	1991	Ex Patterson's, Birmingham, 1995
K805SCC	Leyland-DAF 400	Leyland-DAF	M16	1992	

Previous Registrations:

875EPX	DJB864V	A2NPT	D125HML	D659WEY	D933XWP, 610LYB

Livery: White, red, orange and yellow

OARE'S OF HOLYWELL

G A Oare, Ty Draw, Brynford, Holywell, Flintshire CH8 8LP

ANY586T	Bedford YMT	Plaxton Supreme IV	C53F	1979	Ex Prestatyn Coachways, Dyserth, 1996
SVL172W	Bristol VRT/SL3/6LXB	Eastern Coach Works	H43/31F	1981	Ex RoadCar, 1995
GIL9489	Van Hool T815	Van Hool Alicron	C49FT	1982	Ex Griffiths, Port Dinorwig, 1991
HSV723	Volvo B10M-61	Duple Goldliner IV	C57F	1982	Ex TR Coaches, Wrexham, 1996
FIL3825	DAF SBR2300DHS553	Jonckheere Jubilee P99	CH55/13CT	1982	Ex Crescent, North Walsham, 1992
HUI4199	Van Hool T815	Van Hool Alizée	C53FT	1984	Ex Arvonia, Llanrug, 1995
B991UPS	Volvo B10M-61	Plaxton Paramount 3500	C53FT	1984	Ex Mayne's, Buckie, 1994
D826KBO	Ford Transit VE6	Ford	M14	1985	Ex Phil Henderson, Pen-y-graig, 1993
E710WNE	Freight Rover Sherpa	Made-to-Measure	B16F	1988	Ex Tarporley Travel, 1990
F345ONO	Ford Transit VE6	Dormobile	B20F	1988	Ex Sel's, Llanrwst, 1991
F418DAX	Ford Transit VE6	Premier	M14	1988	Ex Waddon, Bedwas, 1996
F904NBB	Ford Transit VE6	Ford	M12	1989	Ex private owner, 1993

Previous Registrations:

B991UPS	B619AMD, YSU989	GIL9489	FLG776X, UDM96
FIL3825	DLX46Y, 103UTW	HUI4199	A947GPM, 367ARV
HSV723	JBK111X		

Livery: White/cream, yellow, orange and red

Note:- A number of minibuses are operated as non-PCVs in addition to the fleet above

The Nefyn Coaches fleet is replenished regularly, all appearing resplendent in fleet livery. D659WEY, a typical fleet purchase of a late model Bedford with Plaxton bodywork, is seen ready for departure on Bws Ysgol (schoolbus) duties. *John Jones*

Oare's have contracted during the last two years with all bar one double-deck being withdrawn. Representing the coach fleet is this picture of FIL382 , a DAF SBR2300 with Jonckheere Jubilee double-deck body, taken before the new depot building had been built. *John Jones*

OWENS MOTORS

Owen's Motors Ltd, Temeside House, Station Road, Knighton,
Powys, LD7 1DT

OVK907R	Bedford YLQ	Plaxton Supreme III	C45F	1977	Ex Evans, Tregaron, 1989
MSF679T	Bedford YLQ	Plaxton Supreme IV	C45F	1979	Ex Smith's, High Wycombe, 1990
WBX65T	Bedford YMT	Plaxton Supreme IV Express	C53F	1979	Ex Crawshaw, Mansfield, 1989
DFB233W	Bedford YMQ	Plaxton Supreme IV	C33F	1981	Ex Evans, Tregaron, 1993
MCY333X	Bedford YNT	Duple Dominant IV	C53F	1982	Ex Brooklyn, Shirland, 1994
572RKJ	DAF SB2305DHS585	Duple 340	C51FT	1987	Ex Lydford, Holcombe, 1995
NIW8293	LAG G355Z	LAG Panoramic	C49FT	1987	Ex Chameleon Coaches, Bilston, 1994
E712UHB	Bedford YNV Venturer	Duple 320	C57F	1988	Ex Waddon, Bedwas, 1993
G838FTX	Ford Transit VE6	Deansgate	M14	1989	Ex Waddon, Bedwas, 1993
G137TNU	Hestair Duple SDA1512	Duple 425	C55F	1990	Ex Bywater, Rochdale, 1995
J691XUX	DAF 400	Deansgate	M16	1992	

Previous Registrations:

572RKJ	D70NHB		NIW8293	E121KNV

Livery: Blue and grey

Owens Motors is a Welsh operator whose only depot is in England, albeit by a few metres. The town of Knighton sits astride not only the English border but also Offa's Dyke and the Heart of Wales rail line, both of which are important in providing motivation to tourists. Bus services in the area are thin and Owen's market day service to Newtown is almost the only service remaining apart from school contracts. Private hire and holiday demands call for modern coaches, seen here is the newest full-size coach, G137TNU, a Hestair Duple 425 integral. *David Donati*

PADARN.

D C & D C Price, Unit 5, Griffiths Crossing Industrial Estate, Caernarfon, Gwynedd LL55 1TS

NPU981M	Bristol VRT/SL2/6LX	Eastern Coach Works	H39/31F	1973	Ex Express Motors, Bontnewydd, 1994
UTF735M	Leyland Leopard PSU3B/4R	Duple Dominant	C49F	1974	Ex Evans, Tregaron, 1992
WDS115V	Leyland Fleetline FE30AGR	Alexander AD	H44/31F	1980	Ex Clydeside, 1995
C900JGA	Bedford YNT	Plaxton Paramount 3200 II	C53F	1986	Ex Evans, Tregaron, 1995
D104TFT	Freight Rover Sherpa	Carlyle	B18F	1987	Ex Busways, 1989
G358FOP	Iveco Daily 49.10	Carlyle Dailybus	B25F	1990	

Previous Registrations:
WDS115V   HSD71V, WLT364

Livery: Red, grey, white and yellow (coaches); red and grey (buses)

Padarn commenced operating taxis from the town of Llanberis expanding into bus and coach operation in the late 1980s. Expansion, following the award of Bws Gwynedd contracts included a pair of Carlyle-bodied Dennis Darts and Leyland Nationals which have been withdrawn following the loss on re-tendering. Acquired and repainted in 1995 was C900JGA seen here at Griffiths Crossing, near Caernarfon. *Ralph Stevens*

Phillips' longest-serving vehicle, and the last one bought to bus grant specification is OLG601V seen here passing through Mold. Phillips have a share of the Wrexham to Mold service. *John Jones*

Pied Bull are one of the operators who work on Bws Clwyd and its successor authorities' service 26 from Mold as well as route 19 from Mold to Wrexham. Here is seen a Freight Rover Sherpa with Carlyle Citybus 2 bodywork which was one of the final batch of eight for National Welsh. *John Jones*

PHILLIPS

H O, J & A S Phillips, St John's House, Brynford Road,
Holywell, Flintshire CH8 7RP

Depots : Brynford Road, Holywell and Greenfield, Holywell

	XTF467L	Bristol LHL6L	Plaxton Elite III	C51F	1973	Ex Bassetts, Tittensor, 1994
	YYB967N	Bedford YRQ	Plaxton Elite III Express	C45F	1974	Ex Osborne, West Bromwich, 1991
w	MCA613P	Bristol LH6L	Eastern Coach Works	B43F	1975	Ex Crosville, 1983
	MCA614P	Bristol LH6L	Eastern Coach Works	B43F	1975	Ex Crosville, 1983
w	MCA615P	Bristol LH6L	Eastern Coach Works	B43F	1975	Ex Crosville, 1983
	ABV166R	Bedford YMT	Duple Dominant	C53F	1976	Ex Astbury, Mostyn, 1989
	PRN117T	Bedford YMT	Duple Dominant II	C53F	1979	Ex T Williams & Sons, Ponciau, 1995
	XSD602T	Seddon Pennine VII	Alexander AY	DP49F	1978	Ex P&O Lloyd, Bagillt, 1992
	OLG601V	Bedford YMT	Plaxton Supreme IV Express	C53F	1979	
	B679EWE	Bedford YNT	Duple Laser 2	C53F	1985	Ex Whitehead, Conisbrough, 1995
	C830XCJ	Bedford YNT	Duple Laser 2	C53F	1986	
	D761PTU	Freight Rover Sherpa	Dormobile	B16F	1986	Ex Bee Line Buzz, 1990
	D30TKA	Freight Rover Sherpa	Dormobile	B16F	1987	Ex North Western, 1990

Livery: Red and cream

PIED BULL COACHES

R Williams, 53 Woodlands Close, Mold, Flintshire CH7 1UU

Depot : Gas Lane, Mold

CUN669L	Ford R192	Duple Dominant	C45F	1973	Ex Wright, Pencae, 1977
ODM500V	Leyland Leopard PSU3E/4R	Duple Dominant II Express	C49F	1979	Ex Barry Cooper, Stockton Heath, 1990
LIJ6832	Ford R1115	Plaxton Paramount 3200	C49F	1983	Ex Roger Hill, Congleton, 1988
C284AOR	Iveco-Fiat 79.14	Robin Hood	C28FL	1985	Ex Mawbey, Ombersley, 1993
C315DVU	Ford Transit 160	Deansgate	M12	1986	
G278HDW	Freight Rover Sherpa	Carlyle Citybus 2	B20F	1990	Ex Executive Travel, Fenton, 1993

Previous Registrations:
LIJ6832   BLJ711Y

Livery: Blue and white

Apart from a thrice-weekly service in Prestatyn, situated on the north Wales coast, Prestatyn Coachways operate mostly schools duties using a variety of vehicles including this Berkhof Everest-bodied Leyland Tiger that was new to London Country. The Everest is one of the taller single-deck coaches from Berkhof with a height of 3.7 metres, only slightly shorter than the one-and-a-half-deck Emperor at 3.95 metres. B101KPF is seen in Dyserth. *Ralph Stevens*

Two half-hourly services from Bethesda to Bangor are operated by Purple Motors, whose fleet changes during the last two years are confined to revised seating capacities. Here, TMB875R a Leyland Leopard formerly with Chester, was en-route for Bangor when photographed. *Ralph Stevens*

PRESTATYN COACHWAYS

Prestatyn Coachways Ltd, 4 Allt yr Graig, Dyserth, Denbighshire LL18 6DE

Depot :Gwaenysgor Road, Dyserth

RDS250W	Ford R1114	Duple Dominant II	C53F	1980	Ex Reynolds, Gwespyr, 1992
PBO10Y	Ford R1114	Plaxton Supreme V	C53F	1982	Ex Reynolds, Gwespyr, 1992
FDZ4166	Volvo B10M-61	Duple Caribbean	C51FT	1983	Ex Randle, Padiham, 1993
B101KPF	Leyland Tiger TRCTL11/3RH	Berkhof Everest 370	C49FT	1984	Ex Richard Green Travel, Bournemouth, 1994
C433HHL	Bedford YNT	Plaxton Paramount 3200 II	C53F	1985	Ex Happy Times, Wednesfield, 1992
F228BAX	Freight Rover Sherpa	Carlyle Citybus 2	B18F	1989	Ex Red & White, 1994
H14JYM	Mercedes-Benz 609D	Whitaker Europa	B19F	1991	Ex Halton Mini, Runcorn, 1996

Previous Registrations:
FDZ4166   THL294Y

Livery: Blue and/or white

PURPLE MOTORS

S R & H Bright, Castle Garage, Bethesda, Gwynedd, LL57 3ND

HPG31N	Leyland Leopard PSU3B/4R	Duple Dominant	B53F	1975	Ex Safeguard, Guildford, 1982
HEN867N	Leyland Leopard PSU4C/2R	Willowbrook Warrior(1991)	B44F	1975	Ex Chester, 1982
KCO524P	Volvo B58-61	Plaxton Supreme III	C57F	1976	Ex Caelloi, Pwllheli, 1984
TMB875R	Leyland Leopard PSU4D/2R	Duple Dominant	B47F	1976	Ex Chester, 1987
TMB876R	Leyland Leopard PSU4D/2R	Duple Dominant	B47F	1976	Ex Chester, 1987
NSP330R	Ailsa B55-10	Alexander AV	H44/31D	1976	Ex Tayside, 1988
NEY819	Volvo B58-61	Plaxton Viewmaster IV Exp	C53F	1980	Ex Russell, Blackheath, 1985
BEY7W	Bedford YMT	Duple Dominant	B53F	1981	
TNR812X	Bedford YMQ	Duple Dominant IV	C45F	1981	Ex Smith, Kibworth, 1988
GEY389Y	Bedford YNT	Duple Dominant IV	C53F	1982	
HCC852	Leyland Tiger TRCTL11/3R	Plaxton Paramount 3500	C49F	1983	Ex Safeguard, Guildford, 1988
MEY395	Volvo B10M-61	Plaxton Paramount 3500 II	C53F	1986	Ex Wallace Arnold, 1991
D900STU	Leyland Tiger TRCTL11/3RZ	Plaxton Paramount 3200 II	C57F	1987	Ex P&O Lloyd, Bagillt, 1993

Previous Registrations:
HCC852	UTN956Y		MEY395	C120DWR
NEY819	GOP720W			

Livery: Maroon and cream (buses); red, cream and blue (coaches)

RICHARDS BROS

CH, WJM, R & DN Richards, Moylgrove Garage, Pentood Ind Est, Cardigan, SA43 3AD.

Depots :Moylgrove Garage, Pentood Ind Est, Cardigan; Cardigan Road, Newport and Llanungar, Solva

RAA172G	Bedford SB5	Willowbrook	B42F	1969	Ex Ford, Gunnislake, 1982
WJO923K	Bedford SB3	Willowbrook 001	B42F	1972	Ex Oxfordshire HA, 1980
JKO62N	Bedford YRT	Duple Dominant	B53F	1975	Ex Maidstone, 1981
JKO63N	Bedford YRT	Duple Dominant	B53F	1975	Ex Maidstone, 1981
JKO64N	Bedford YRT	Duple Dominant	B53F	1975	Ex Maidstone, 1981
GPA853N	Bedford YRQ	Duple Dominant	B45F	1975	Ex Purley Car, Warlingham, 1980
HPB674N	Bedford YRQ	Duple Dominant	B47F	1975	Ex Marchwood, Haverfordwest, 1981
TPX332P	Bedford YRQ	Duple Dominant	DP45F	1975	Ex Marchwood, Haverfordwest, 1981
NKE304P	Bedford YRT	Duple Dominant	B53F	1976	Ex Maidstone, 1982
NKE305P	Bedford YRT	Duple Dominant	B53F	1976	Ex Maidstone, 1982
NKE306P	Bedford YRT	Duple Dominant	B53F	1976	Ex Maidstone, 1982
LVS433P	Bedford YLQ	Plaxton Supreme III	C41F	1976	Ex Stanley, Hersham, 1985
LDE547P	Bedford YLQ	Duple Dominant	B47F	1976	
VUP745R	Bedford YLQ	Duple Dominant	B47F	1977	Ex Wilson, Middlesbrough, 1988
YDE350	Bedford YMT	Willowbrook Warrior (1988)	B51F	1977	Ex Safeway, Dagenham, 1988
OBX345R	Bedford YLQ	Duple Dominant I	C45F	1977	
OBX346R	Bedford YLQ	Duple Dominant I	C45F	1977	

Opposite: **Even though there have been significant arrivals in the fleet, the Bedford/Duple Dominant bus still features significantly in the fleet. XNN890Y is the latest of the type and was acquired from national Plant and Transport in 1991. It is seen in Finch's Square, Cardigan.** *John Jones*
Richard Brothers was the first Welsh operator to place into service the Optare Vecta-bodied MAN 11.190 chassis though four further examples have been taken into stock at Crosville Cymru. M197CDE is seen in the fading light of early March as it waits time in Fishguard while working between Haverfordwest and Cardigan. *John Jones*

Richards Bros continue to sell older Willowbrook bodied Bedfords, now only two SBs remain. The Duple Dominant bus body is still largely in evidence with some nineteen in use representing the full production period. The oldest purchased new is now LDE547P, seen here in Finch Square, Cardiff. *John Jones*

Richards' continued investment in modern vehicles was assisted by the purchase of two second-hand Optare Delta buses that joined the one delivered in 1990. G837LWR, formerly a demonstrator, introduced a silver-based livery to the fleet and, since then, all DpTAC qualifying vehicles have been repainted to match. The other second-hand Delta came from airport duties at Gatwick and is seen at Richards Newport base. *John Jones*

Plaxton Pointer-bodied Dennis Dart, L485XDE was Richards' second of the chassis type and is seen on an afternoon school contract. *John Jones*

RGS99R	Bedford YLQ	Plaxton Supreme III	C41F	1977	Ex Stanley, Hersham, 1985
BBR738S	Bedford YMT	Duple Dominant	B53F	1977	Ex Barwick, Barlow, 1990
RDE681S	Bedford YLQ	Plaxton Supreme III Express	C45F	1978	
DTT496T	Bedford YMT	Duple Dominant	B53F	1979	Ex Berkeley, Paulton, 1992
FFW508T	Bedford YMT	Duple Dominant	B55F	1979	Ex Evans, Tregaron, 1994
YCV155T	Bedford YLQ	Duple Dominant	B45F	1979	Ex Western National, 1989
YPB828T	Bedford YMT	Duple Dominant II	C53F	1979	Ex Lewis, Llanrhystyd, 1988
HVC9V	Bedford YMT	Plaxton Supreme IV	C53F	1979	Ex Gastonia, Cranleigh, 1984
ADE612V	Bedford YMT	Plaxton Supreme IV Express	C53F	1979	
BBX190V	Bedford YMT	Plaxton Supreme IV Express	C53F	1980	
JTM114V	Bedford YMT	Duple Dominant	B55F	1980	Ex Stanley, Hersham, 1985
LVO801W	Bedford YLQ	Duple Dominant II	C45F	1980	Ex Evans, Dinas Mawddwy, 1994
MCH352W	Bedford YMT	Duple Dominant	B53F	1981	Ex National Plant & Transport, 1991
RVO839X	Bedford YMT	Duple Dominant	B53F	1981	Ex National Plant & Transport, 1991
XNN890Y	Bedford YMT	Duple Dominant	B53F	1983	Ex National Plant & Transport, 1991
NDE481Y	Bedford CF	Dormobile	M12	1983	
RBO350	Volvo B10M-61	Plaxton Paramount 3500	C49FT	1983	
RBO202	Volvo B10M-61	Plaxton Paramount 3500	C49FT	1984	
C334GTH	Bedford CF	Dormobile	M12	1985	Ex Ridler, Dulverton, 1990
D44AVJ	Bedford CF	Dormobile	M12	1986	
D982OEJ	DAF SB2300DHS585	Duple 340	C53FT	1986	
D983OEJ	DAF SB2300DHS585	Duple 340	C53FT	1986	
RBO284	DAF SB2300DHS585	Duple 340	C53FT	1986	
E36RBO	Renault-Dodge S56	Reeve Burgess Beaver	B25F	1987	Ex Newport, 1991
E788MDE	Volvo B10M-61	Plaxton Paramount 3500 III	C49FT	1988	
F876RDE	Mercedes-Benz 609D	Reeve Burgess Beaver	C19F	1988	
F566ABV	Freight Rover Sherpa	Elme Orion	B21F	1989	Ex Bellview Cs, Paisley, 1993
F133UDE	DAF MB230LT615	Plaxton Paramount 3500 III	C51FT	1989	
F334FWW	DAF SB220LC550	Optare Delta	DP48F	1989	Ex BAA, Gatwick, 1994
G837LWR	DAF SB220LC550	Optare Delta	B49F	1990	Ex Optare demonstrator, 1992
G978KJX	DAF SB3000DKV601	Van Hool Alizée	C53F	1990	Ex Smith, Alcester, 1992
H704FDE	DAF SB220LC550	Optare Delta	B49F	1990	
H158HDE	Dennis Dart 9.8SDL3004	Carlyle Dartline	B35F	1991	
H332FEJ	Volkswagen Microbus 252	Devon Conversions	M9	1990	
J64PDE	Volvo B10M-60	Jonckheere Deauville P599	C51FT	1992	
K530RJX	DAF SB3000DKVF601	Van Hool Alizée	C51FT	1993	Ex C&H Coaches, Fleetwood, 1994
L485XDE	Dennis Dart 9.8SDL3035	Plaxton Pointer	B40F	1994	
M197CDE	MAN 11.190	Optare Vecta	B40F	1994	
M591CDE	LDV 400	LDV	M16	1995	
M680DDE	Mercedes-Benz 811D	Marshall C16	B31F	1995	
M740DDE	Dennis Dart 9.8SDL3040	Plaxton Pointer	B40F	1995	
M798DDE	DAF SB3000WS601	Van Hool Alizée	C51FT	1995	

Previous Registrations:

RBO202	A85GEJ	RBO350	NDE760Y
RBO284	C785CDE	YDE350	TMJ952R

Livery: White, blue and maroon; silver and blue (DpTAC Buses); white, red, black and silver (Executive coaches)

The original Dart, with Carlyle Dartline body has notched up five years service, much of it on the main 412 Cardigan to Haverfordwest service which passes through Fishguard. Photographed passing the Newport depot when heading north is H158HDE. *John Jones*

ROGERS

E E & C B Rogers, 4 Maeshyfryd, Graigfechan, Denbighshire LL15 2ET

FUY812J	Bedford YRQ	Plaxton Elite II	C45F	1971	Ex Bob Edwards, Llandegla, 1983
OCA618M	Bedford YRQ	Duple Dominant	C45F	1973	
ACA189S	Bedford YLQ	Plaxton Supreme III	C45F	1977	Ex Hanmers, Wrexham, 1979
OOS923V	Bedford YMT	Plaxton Supreme IV	C53F	1980	Ex King, Kirkcowan, 1985
D165KDN	Volkswagen LT55	Optare City Pacer	B25F	1986	Ex Crosville Cymru, 1990
D434BCJ	Bedford YNT	Plaxton Paramount 3200 III	C53F	1987	Ex Yeomans, Hereford, 1991

Livery: Fawn and orange

ROYAL MAIL POST BUS

The Post Office, South West & South Wales Division, 29 Central Park Avenue,
Plymouth, Devon, PL1 1AA
The Post Office, North Wales & North West Division, 2 Western Road, Crewe,
Cheshire, CW1 1AA

Depots :Post Offices at Abergavenny, Aberystwyth, Builth Wells, Llandovery, Llandrindod Wells, Llanidloes, Machynlleth, Newtown and Welshpool

1750005	J823VUJ	Leyland-DAF 200	Post Office	M11	1992	Llandrindod Wells (R)
1750008	J826VUJ	Leyland-DAF 200	Post Office	M11	1992	Llanidloes - Llangurig
1750011	J825VUJ	Leyland-DAF 200	Post Office	M11	1992	Llanidloes - Dylife
1750029	J824VUJ	Leyland-DAF 200	Post Office	M11	1992	Aberystwyth - Cwmystwyth
1750060	J771VFA	Leyland-DAF 200	Post Office	M10	1992	Builth Wells - Abergwesyn
1760018	J841VUJ	Peugeot 405GLD		M4	1992	Machynlleth - Aberhosan
1760024	J133UUH	Peugeot 405GLD		M4	1992	Abergavenny - Skenfrith
2750007	K457BRE	Leyland-DAF 200	Post Office	M10	1992	Aberystwyth - Blaenpennal
2750008	K698BFA	Leyland-DAF 200	Post Office	M10	1992	Llandrindod Wells - Llaithddu
2750009	K498BRE	Leyland-DAF 200	Post Office	M10	1992	Newtown (R)
2750010	K703BFA	Leyland-DAF 200	Post Office	M10	1992	Newtown - New Mills
2750011	K699BFA	Leyland-DAF 200	Post Office	M10	1992	Builth Wells - Painscastle
2750016	K856CEH	Leyland-DAF 400	Post Office	M14	1993	Llandrindod Wells - Rhayader
2750018	K665EEH	Leyland-DAF 200	Post Office	M10	1993	Welshpool - Foel
2750022	K511WTT	Leyland-DAF 200	Post Office	M10	1993	Llandovery - Rhandirmwyn
2750028	M979HDV	LDV 200	Post Office	M10	1994	Pembroke Dock - Bosherton
2750029	M980HDV	LDV 200	Post Office	M10	1994	Narberth - Landshipping
2750031	L128VEG	LDV 200	Post Office	M10	1994	Pembroke Dock - Angle
2750033	M981HDV	LDV 200	Post Office	M10	1994	Narbeth - Lawrenny
2750035	M487TBF	LDV 200	Post Office	M10	1994	Aberystwyth - Aberffrwd
4750006	M520MTT	LDV 200	Post Office	M10	1994	Tenby (R)

Livery: Post Office red and yellow.

Rogers are based in the village of Graigfechan, about four kilometres south of Ruthin at the southern end of the Vale of Clwyd. The small fleet is employed on typical rural work and it is no surprise that light-weight chassis, here supplied by Bedford, have been used. ACA189S *(above)* was new to Hanmers of Wrexham and joined Rogers when just two years old. This Bedford YLQ carries a Plaxton Supreme III body. The flagship of the fleet is D434BCJ, a YNT model with Plaxton Paramount 3200 mark III body. It is photographed at the Royal Welsh Show at Llanelwedd, Builth Wells.
John Jones/David Donati

SELS MINI TRAVEL

J S Jones, 5 Station Yard, Abergele Road, Llanrwst,
Conwy LL26 0EH

RCC512S	Ford R1114	Duple Dominant II Express	C53F	1978	Ex Griffiths, Port Dinorwig, 1995
OPO899S	Ford Transit	Dormobile	M16	1978	Ex Kirkby Stephen Mini Coaches, 1994
RGE901W	Ford R1014	Plaxton Supreme IV	C45F	1980	Ex Torr's Coaches, Gedling, 1995
VRN44Y	Iveco-Fiat 79-13	Imperial	C23F	1983	Ex Cruickshank, Ellon, 1991
D28KAX	Iveco Daily 49-10	Robin Hood City Nippy	B21F	1986	Ex Dickson of Erskine, 1995
D30KAX	Iveco Daily 49-10	Robin Hood City Nippy	B21F	1986	Ex Dickson of Erskine, 1995
D30BVV	Iveco Daily 49-10	Robin Hood City Nippy	B19F	1987	Ex United Counties, 1994
D506MJA	Iveco Daily 49-10	Robin Hood City Nippy	B21F	1987	Ex GM Buses, 1992
E522TOV	Iveco Daily 49-10	Carlyle Dailybus 2	B25F	1988	Ex Baker, Weston-super-Mare, 1994
F201JGH	Iveco Daily 49-10	Elme Orion	C21F	1989	
G255PGN	Iveco Daily 49-10	Elme Orion	C25F	1990	

Livery: White, yellow and green

SELWYN HUGHES

JS Hughes, Brodawel, Wesley Street, Llanfair Caereinion, Powys SY21 0RX

LUX520P	Bedford YMT	Duple Dominant	C53F	1976	Ex Jones, Meifod, 1990
DNT465T	Bedford YMT	Plaxton Supreme IV	C49F	1979	Ex Davis, Cardington, 1990
A594GWM	Mercedes-Benz LP813	Imperial	C29F	1984	
B624DEV	Ford Transit 160	Ford	M12	1985	Ex Ford Motor Co, Dagenham, 1986
SEL813	Leyland Tiger TRCTL11/3R	Van Hool Alizée	C53F	1986	Ex Everyman's Coaches, Maudlin, 1987
D243PAW	Mercedes-Benz 709D	Hughes	C18F	1987	Ex van, 1987
SEL219	LAG G355Z	LAG Panoramic	C49FT	1988	
F209PNR	DAF MB230LB615	Caetano Algarve	C49FT	1989	
H195CVU	Leyland-DAF 400	Made-to-Measure	M16	1990	
H831AHS	Volvo B10M-60	Plaxton Paramount 3500 III	C53F	1991	Ex Park's, 1993
H154DVM	Scania K113CRB	Van Hool Alizée	C49FT	1991	Ex Shearings, 1994
J111SEL	Mazda E2200	Howletts	M15	1992	
L725JUX	Leyland-DAF 400	Leyland-DAF	M16	1994	

Previous Registrations:

DNT465T	DRW912T, 3063VC	SEL219	E671NNV	SEL813	C674BCR

Livery: Beige and orange

Sels have accumulated a number of Iveco minibuses for a range of duties while two coaches are operated in addition. Smaller of the two is a 10-metre Ford, RGE901W, photographed when it was parked near their depot at North Llanrwst rail station, a request stop for trains on the Blaenau Ffestiniog - Llandudno line. *John Jones*

Selwyn Hughes is based in the town of Llanfair Caereinion on the A458 between Welshpool and Dolgellau. This rural area has few scheduled services, the only notable being a Post Bus from Welshpool. Schools and private hire are provided by Selwyns whose Caetano-bodied DAF, F209PNR is seen here. *John Jones*

SILCOX

Silcox Motor Coach Company Ltd, Waterloo Garage, Pembroke Dock,
Pembrokeshire SA72 4RR

Depot :Waterloo Garage, Pembroke Dock; North End Car Park, Tenby and Milford Docks, Milford Haven

WHN411G	Bristol VRT/SL2/6LX	Eastern Coach Works	H39/31F	1969	Ex South Wales, 1986
WCD524K	Bristol VRT/SL2/6LX	Eastern Coach Works	H39/31F	1971	Ex Southdown, 1986
KDE161L	Leyland Leopard PSU3B/4R	Duple Dominant Express	C49F	1972	Ex Worthington, Collingham, 1987
AJA418L	Bristol VRT/SL2/6LX	Eastern Coach Works	H43/32F	1973	Ex Stevensons, 1987
AJA421L	Bristol VRT/SL2/6LX	Eastern Coach Works	H43/32F	1973	Ex Stevensons, 1987
109CUF	Leyland Leopard PSU5/4R	Willowbrook Warrior (1988)	B61F	1973	Ex Glyn Williams, Crosskeys, 1992
PDE570M	Leyland Leopard PSU3B/4R	Plaxton Elite III Express	C51F	1974	
HWY719N	Leyland Leopard PSU3B/4R	Willowbrook Warrior (1988)	B55F	1975	Ex Glyn Williams, Crosskeys, 1992
GSK676	Leyland Leopard PSU3B/4R	Willowbrook Warrior (1988)	B55F	1975	Ex Glyn Williams, Crosskeys, 1992
GNL839N	Leyland Leopard PSU3C/4R	Alexander AY	DP62F	1975	Ex Minsterley Motors, 1991
GNL840N	Leyland Leopard PSU3C/4R	Alexander AY	B62F	1975	Ex Jones, Malvern, 1991
HDE250N	Leyland Leopard PSU3C/4R	Duple Dominant	B65F	1975	
HDE611N	Leyland Leopard PSU3C/4R	Duple Dominant Express	C53F	1975	
HDE612N	Leyland Leopard PSU3C/4R	Plaxton Elite III Express	C53F	1975	
HDE617N	Leyland Leopard PSU3C/4R	Plaxton Elite III Express	C53F	1975	
MHS19P	Leyland Leopard PSU3/3R	Alexander AYS	B53F	1975	Ex Perry, Bromyard, 1990
KTT40P	Bristol LH6L	Eastern Coach Works	B45F	1976	Ex NCB, Rotherham, 1985
PVO624	Leyland Leopard PSU3C/4R	Plaxton Supreme III	C53F	1976	Ex Stephenson, Rochford, 1992
LDE163P	Leyland Leopard PSU3C/4R	Duple Dominant Express	C53F	1976	
LDE164P	Leyland Leopard PSU3C/4R	Duple Dominant Express	C53F	1976	
LDE165P	Bristol LH6L	Duple Dominant	B47F	1976	
LDE166P	Bristol LH6L	Duple Dominant	B47F	1976	
MHX530P	Leyland Leopard PSU3C/4R	Duple Dominant	C53F	1976	Ex Evans, Tregaron, 1987
OSJ622R	Leyland Leopard PSU3C/3R	Alexander AY	B53F	1977	Ex United, 1991
OSJ623R	Leyland Leopard PSU3C/3R	Alexander AY	B53F	1977	Ex Minsterley Motors, 1991
NDE86R	Leyland Leopard PSU3C/4R	Duple Dominant	B65F	1977	
VAW527	Leyland Leopard PSU3D/4R	Willowbrook Crusader (1989)	C51F	1977	Ex Perry, Bromyard, 1989
BUR712S	Leyland Leopard PSU3E/4R	Duple Dominant	DP53F	1978	Ex Stephenson, Rochford, 1992
9195PU	Leyland Leopard PSU3E/4R	Duple Dominant	C57F	1978	Ex Lattimore, Markyate, 1992
KSU409	Leyland Leopard PSU3E/4R	Plaxton Supreme III	C53F	1978	Ex Hants & Dorset, 1983
817FKH	Leyland Leopard PSU3E/4R	Plaxton Supreme III	C53F	1978	Ex South Wales, 1987
538OHU	Leyland Leopard PSU4E/4R	Plaxton Supreme IV	C45F	1979	Ex Bicknell, Godalming1983
WBX870T	Leyland Leopard PSU3E/4R	Duple Dominant II Express	C53F	1979	
WBX871T	Leyland Leopard PSU3E/4R	Duple Dominant II Express	C53F	1979	
804SHW	Leyland Leopard PSU5C/4R	Duple Dominant II	C57F	1979	
CWG707V	Leyland Atlantean AN68A/1R	Alexander AL	H45/29D	1979	Ex Camms, Nottingham, 1993
CWG712V	Leyland Atlantean AN68A/1R	Alexander AL	H45/29D	1979	Ex Camms, Nottingham, 1993
CWG759V	Leyland Atlantean AN68A/1R	Roe	H45/29D	1979	Ex Camms, Nottingham, 1993
BBX915V	Leyland Leopard PSU3E/4R	Duple Dominant II Express	C53F	1980	
BDE140V	Leyland Leopard PSU3E/4R	Duple Dominant	B63F	1980	
BDE143V	Leyland Leopard PSU3E/4R	Duple Dominant II Express	C53F	1980	
GNF13V	Leyland Titan TNTL11/1RF	Park Royal	H47/26F	1980	Ex Capital Citybus, 1995
EHW294W	Volvo B58-61	Duple Dominant II	C55F	1981	Ex Kerricabs, Newport, 1994
A12WLS	DAF SB2300DHS585	Plaxton Paramount 3500	C53F	1984	Ex Travelfar, Henfield, 1992
A14WLS	Volvo B10M-61	Caetano Algarve	C49FT	1985	Ex Agenalink, Dundee, 1992

Opposite, top: **Leyland Leopards are still to be found in large numbers in the Silcox fleet, several with
refurbished Duple Dominant bodies that no longer carry the chrome trim. One example is 9195PU
which originally worked on National Express, and is now seen in Cardiff.** *John Jones*
Opposite, bottom: **Part of the regular intake of buses into the Silcox fleet has included four Dennis
Darts and ten Mercedes-Benz minibuses. One of the latter is M361CDE, a 709 model with WS
Coachbuilders bodywork. It was working local services when photographed in Tenby in February
1996.** *John Jones*

Just three Bristol saloons remain in the Silcox fleet and only one carries the more common Eastern Coach Works body. The survivor is KTT40P which arrived with Silcox after being used by the then NCB for transporting miners. *John Jones*

Bws Dyfed support to improve the vehicles used on their services has been incorporated into the tendering. In the 1994 round Silcox added four Dennis Darts to the fleet to run the contracts awarded. Three of these were Marshall-bodied 9-metre versions while the fourth was a 9.8-metre East Lancashire example, M174BDE. *Malc McDonald*

To increase the proportion of number of vehicles in the fleet that meet DpTAC specification, Mercedes-Benz F559UDE found itself out of favour and was sold while the book was in preparation. Before it left it was photographed outside the town walls of Tenby.
John Jones

A9WLS	DAF SB2300DHS585	Plaxton Paramount 3200 II	C53F	1985	
A11WLS	DAF SB2300DHS585	Plaxton Paramount 3200 II	C55F	1986	
A7WLS	DAF SB2300DHS585	Plaxton Paramount 3200 II	C49F	1986	
D854CKV	Iveco Daily 49.10	Robin Hood City Nippy	B21F	1987	Ex Stagecoach Midland Red, 1996
F865DAC	Iveco Daily 49.10	Robin Hood City Nippy	B21F	1988	Ex Stagecoach Midland Red, 1996
F580OOU	Iveco Daily 49.10	Dormobile	B23F	1988	Ex City Line, 1996
F585OOU	Iveco Daily 49.10	Dormobile	B23F	1988	Ex City Line, 1996
A2WLS	Duple 425 SDA1512	Duple	C55FT	1988	
A15WLS	Volvo B10M-61	Plaxton Paramount 3200 III	C57F	1988	Ex Frames Rickards, Brentford, 1992
A8WLS	LAG Panoramic G355Z	LAG	C49FT	1988	Ex Berryhurst, London, 1992
A3WLS	Volvo B10M-60	Van Hool Alizée	C53F	1989	Ex Travellers, Hounslow, 1994
A4WLS	Volvo B10M-60	Van Hool Alizée	C49FT	1989	Ex Gain Travel, Wibsey, 1994
A5WLS	LAG Panoramic G355Z	LAG	C49FT	1989	Ex Henderson, Crewe, 1992
A6WLS	Volvo B10M-60	Caetano Algarve	C53F	1989	Ex Darry, Broughton, 1996
H736EDE	Mercedes-Benz 709D	Dormobile Routemaker	B29F	1990	
H743EDE	Mercedes-Benz 709D	Dormobile Routemaker	B29F	1990	
H754EDE	Mercedes-Benz 709D	Dormobile Routemaker	B29F	1990	
H227GDE	Mercedes-Benz 711D	Dormobile Routemaker	B33F	1991	
J387ODE	Mercedes-Benz 811D	Crystals	B31F	1992	
K651TDE	Mercedes-Benz 709D	Crystals	B33F	1992	
M174BDE	Dennis Dart 9.8SDL3040	East Lancashire	B40F	1994	
M16SMC	Dennis Dart 9SDL3053	Marshall C36	DP31F	1994	
M17SMC	Dennis Dart 9SDL3053	Marshall C36	DP31F	1994	
M18SMC	Dennis Dart 9SDL3053	Marshall C36	DP31F	1994	
M361CDE	Mercedes-Benz 709D	WS Wessex II	B27F	1994	
M368CDE	Mercedes-Benz 709D	Mellor	B27F	1994	
M674CDE	Mercedes-Benz 709D	Mellor	B27F	1994	

Previous Registrations:

109CUF	NGV288M	A15WLS	E167OMD	A8WLS	F628SRP
538OHU	AJD162T	A16WLS	-	A9WLS	B538XDE,PVO624
804SHW	YBX608V	A2WLS	E522MDE	BUR712S	XWX169S,FIL6784
817FKH	AFH182T	A3WLS	F552TMH	GSK676	HWY720N
9195PU	WFH166S	A4WLS	F866XJX	KDE161L	VCW1L
A11WLS	VAW527	A5WLS	G994FVV	KSU409	WFH170S
A12WLS	A263BTY, 9195PU	A6WLS	G903WAY	PVO624	LMA59P
A14WLS	B722MBC	A7WLS	C392CDE,109CUF	VAW527	OKY54R

Livery: Red and cream (buses); cream, red and blue (coaches)

SILVER STAR

Silver Star Coach Holidays Ltd, 13 Castle Square, Caernarfon, Gwynedd, LL55 2NF

Depots: Rhosgadfan, Upper Llandwrog; Cibyn Industrial Estate, Caernarfon

JWU335J	Bristol RELL6G	Eastern Coach Works	DP50F	1971	Ex Ashville College, Harrogate, 1987
YFM269L	Bristol RELL6G	Eastern Coach Works	B50F	1973	Ex Catch-a-Bus, East Boldon, 1995
BNE765N	Bristol LH6L	Eastern Coach Works	B43F	1974	Ex Richardson, Sheffield, 1985
GTX359N	Bristol RESL6G	Eastern Coach Works	B47F	1974	Ex Catch-a-Bus, East Boldon, 1995
GTX361N	Bristol RESL6G	Eastern Coach Works	B47F	1975	Ex Catch-a-Bus, East Boldon, 1995
LHL245P	Leyland Leopard PSU3C/4R	Alexander AT	DP51F	1976	Ex Graham's, Talke, 1993
OJD68R	Bristol LH6L	Eastern Coach Works	B39F	1977	Ex Trimdon Motor Services, 1990
OJD87R	Bristol LH6L	Eastern Coach Works	B39F	1977	Ex Trimdon Motor Services, 1990
SNU852R	Bristol LH6L	Eastern Coach Works	B45F	1977	Ex East Midland, 1989
SLO514R	Bedford YMT	Duple Dominant I	C53F	1977	Ex Fox, Hayes, 1981
WVO855S	Bristol LH6L	Eastern Coach Works	DP37F	1978	Ex Bluebird, 1993
YBF681S	Bedford VRT/SL3/501	Eastern Coach Works	H43/31F	1978	Ex PMT, 1993
WCC92V	Bedford YMT	Plaxton Supreme IV Express	C53F	1980	
OCC993	Volvo B10M-61	Plaxton Viewmaster IV	C49FT	1982	Ex Baker, Biddulph, 1988
D211GLJ	Freight Rover Sherpa 385	Dormobile	B16F	1987	Ex London Country SW, 1990
E911UNW	Volvo B10M-61	Plaxton Paramount 3500 III	C48FT	1988	Ex Wallace Arnold, 1992
H606UWR	Volvo B10M-60	Plaxton Paramount 3500 III	C50F	1991	Ex Wallace Arnold, 1994
J198PEY	Dennis Dart 9.8SDL3012	Plaxton Pointer	B40F	1992	
N1EDW	Volvo B10M-62	Van Hool Alizée	C49FT	1996	

Previous Registrations:
OCC993   9995RU, XBF1X

Livery: Blue and cream (buses); green (most coaches).

Silver Star's fleet of Bristols has expanded since 1994 with the arrival of three REs from Catch-a-Bus. The LH stock has remained unchanged with the oldest, flat-fronted BNE765N, seen passing the new bus station in Caernarfon. *John Jones*

In addition to the new arrivals, the re-instatement, after several years of restoration, of JWU335J provided a numerical boost to the RE fleet. There are now four of the type, two long and two 10-metre. *John Jones*

Leyland-engined Bristol VR, YBF681S, is pictured at Cesarea above Carmel in the tangled network of settlements and hamlets served by Silver Star. It is instructive to compare the Ordnance Survey map of the area with that produced by Bws Gwynedd to see how few names appear the same on both. *John Jones*

It is pleasing to see vehicles with a full complement of wheel trims when they are in service and not just for rally or Concours events. Seen here, YMB508W has recently been joined by another series 3 example JAZ9864. Series 1 NUD105L will, however, soon go. *John Jones*

Stratos Travel specialise in holiday work and maintain a fleet to match the requirement. The first vehicle operated in 1982 was a Bova and, with few exceptions, these have remained the preferred choice since. Vehicles are normally supplied new with only three, and the Austin CXB, being operated elsewhere first. The latest addition to the fleet is N255XNT which has displaced the first Futura in the fleet. The Austin CXB is currently in storage at Newtown awaiting the opportunity to return it to service. *David Donati*

STRAFFORD'S COACHES

G A Strafford, Units 7 & 8, Five Crosses Industrial Estate, Coedpoeth, Wrexham LL11 3RD

NUD105L	Bristol VRT/SL/6G	Eastern Coach Works	DPH38/30F	1973	Ex Dyma-Fo, Minera, 1988
TXI2443	Volvo B58-61	Plaxton Viewmaster IV	C51F	1980	Ex Ashton, St Helens, 1989
BEN271V	Bedford YMT	Duple Dominant	C53F	1980	Ex Dyma-Fo, Minera, 1988
SJI5620	Bristol LHS6L	Plaxton Supreme IV	C30F	1981	Ex Dial-a-Cab, Callington, 1994
JAZ9864	Bristol VRT/SL3/6LXB	Eastern Coach Works	H43/31F	19..	Ex ??, 1996
YMB508W	Bristol VRT/SL3/6LXB	Eastern Coach Works	H43/31F	1981	Ex Crosville Cymru, 1991
NJI9478	Leyland Tiger TRCTL11/3R	Plaxton Paramount 3500	C53F	1983	Ex Swansdown Coaches, Inkpen, 1994
TJI7518	Van Hool T815	Van Hool Alizée	C49FT	1984	Ex Barrie Patterson, Seahouses, 1995
SJI5619	Mercedes-Benz 811D	Coachcraft	C20F	1987	Ex Mansfield, Swindon, 1995
D165NON	Freight Rover Sherpa	Carlyle	B18F	1987	Ex Bee Line Buzz, 1992

Previous Registrations:

JAZ9864	??	SJI5620	XGO226W, 24GRM, BTU220W
NJI9478	JNM757Y	TJI7518	A514HBC, LAT25S
SJI5619	D246ABV	TXI2443	ATE811V

Livery: White, tan and orange.

STRATOS TRAVEL

JL, JE, CL & KL Jones, Pool Road, Newtown, Powys SY16 1DL

FSU508	Austin CXB	Mellor	C29F	1950	Ex preservation, 1981
KSU477	LAG E180Z	LAG EOS	C53FT	1990	
KSU490	Toyota Coaster HDB30R	Caetano Optimo II	C18F	1991	
K812EET	Bova FHD12.290	Bova Futura	C49FT	1993	Ex Bruce, Shotts, 1994
K123DNT	Bova FHD12.290	Bova Futura	C49FT	1993	
N255XNT	Bova FHD12.340	Bova Futura	C49FT	1996	

Previous Registrations:

FSU508	KYE782	KSU477	G810LVV
KSU476	A422CUJ	KSU490	H173EJF

Livery: Silver and blue

SUMMERDALE

DG & BJL Davies and GR Jones, Summerdale Garage, Letterston,
Pembrokeshire SA62 5UB

OAX335M	Ford R1014	Plaxton Elite III	C45F	1973	Ex Williams, Neath Abbey, 1987
RGF295P	Ford R1014	Plaxton Elite III	C45F	1976	Ex Brown's of Builth, Builth Wells, 1992
WWL439T	Ford R1114	Plaxton Supreme III	C53F	1978	Ex Evans, Tregaron, 1993
WGR144V	Ford R1014	Plaxton Supreme IV	C45F	1980	Ex Bennett, Tamworth, 1994
VJU259X	Ford R1114	Plaxton Supreme VI Express	C53F	1982	Ex Ffoshelig Motors, Newchurch, 1987
OKY76X	Leyland Tiger TRCTL11/3R	Plaxton Supreme V	C46FT	1982	Ex Kerricabs, Newport, 1994
OBO631X	Leyland Tiger TRCTL11/2R	Plaxton Supreme V	C51F	1982	Ex Evans, Tregaron, 1992
PMB287Y	Ford R1114	Duple Dominant IV	C53F	1982	Ex Walkers, Anderton, 1995
VWA66Y	Mercedes-Benz L207D	Whittaker	M12	1983	Ex Seward, Dalwood, 1993
C458BHY	Ford Transit 190	Dormobile	B16F	1985	Ex Athelstan, Chippenham, 1991
D621SJX	DAF MB230DKFL615	Plaxton Paramount 3500 II	C53F	1986	Ex Evans, Tregaron, 1994
H26ARK	Mercedes-Benz 408D	North West Coach Sales	M15	1990	Ex MCH, Uxbridge, 1993

Previous Registrations:

H26ARK	H702ELX, MCH957	PMB287Y	LDM72Y, 848AFM	WWL439T	HLG202T, 551DJB

Livery: Yellow and blue

Summerdale Coaches is named after the garage in Letterston where minibus operations started in 1967. It is located on the main A40 road some eight kilometres south of the west Wales port of Fishguard. The fleet had mostly comprised Fords until the 1990s and representing these is OAX335M, a 10 metre Ford with Plaxton Elite III body. *David Donati*

Summerdale have only recently commenced local service work following the award of Sunday workings on the St David's - Fishguard leg of the Bws Dyfed integrated 411/412/550 service. Shown here on the 412 route is WWL439T which originated with Gold Star, St Asaph after which it spent some time based in Oxfordshire. *Vernon Morgan*

Flagship of the Summerdale fleet is Plaxton Paramount-bodied DAF, D621SJX. The current fleet livery was adopted in 1987 following the purchase of a former Ffoshelig Motors coach in their scheme when that operator was changing to the cream and brown livery. *David Donati*

Under local government reorganisation the rural area around Llansilin and Llangedwyn in the former District of Glyndwr passed to Powys on 1st April 1996. The only operator affected was Tanat Valley whose once light-weight fleet is now dominated by minibuses and Leyland products. Former London Buses CityPacer D368JUM is seen in Shropshire on an Oswestry town service. *Ralph Stevens*

The PMT Bursley body though, now ceased production, carries unconventional lines in an attempt to remove the bread-van image of the early minibuses. Seen at Llanrhaeadr ym Mochnant in service with Tanat Valley is D421FEH. *John Jones*

TANAT VALLEY

R E, P W & R M Morris, The Garage, Pentrefelin, Llangedwyn, Powys SY10 9LE

Depots :The Garage, Pentrefelin; Tanat Valley Garage, Llanrhaeadr ym Mochnant

ABR778S	Leyland Leopard PSU3E/4R	Plaxton Derwent	B60F	1973	Ex Perry, Bromyard, 1992
OEM797S	Leyland Atlantean AN68/1R	MCW	H43/32F	1978	Ex Lofty's, Bridge Trafford, 1994
KRN107T	Leyland Leopard PSU3E/4R	Duple Dominant II Express	C47F	1978	Ex Kinch, Barrow-on-Soar, 1993
KRN111T	Leyland Leopard PSU3E/4R	Duple Dominant II Express	C47F	1979	Ex Kinch, Barrow-on-Soar, 1993
BRC140T	Leyland Leopard PSU3E/4R	Plaxton Supreme III Express	C49F	1979	Ex Dalybus, Eccles, 1995
CWG748V	Leyland Atlantean AN68A/1R	Roe	H45/29D	1979	Ex South Yorkshire's Transport, 1991
HSD78V	Leyland Fleetline FE30AGR	Alexander AD	H44/31F	1980	Ex Clydeside, 1995
HSD84V	Leyland Fleetline FE30AGR	Alexander AD	H44/31F	1980	Ex Clydeside, 1995
SSO448X	Fiat 60F10	Ascough	C25F	1981	Ex Stephenson's, Easingwold, 1995
URC158X	Leyland Leopard PSU3F/4R	Willowbrook 003	C46F	1981	Ex Trent, 1992
SCH148X	Leyland Leopard PSU3F/4R	Willowbrook 003	C49F	1982	Ex Trent, 1992
MAB181X	Bedford YNT	Duple Dominant IV	C49FT	1982	Ex Jones, Llansilin, 1993
ANA91Y	Leyland Leopard PSU5E/4R	Eastern Coach Works B51	DP53F	1982	Ex Reynolds, Watford, 1996
OIB5647	Bova EL28/581	Duple Calypso	C53F	1984	Ex Galloway, Mendlesham, 1990
A385XGG	Aüwaerter Neoplan N122/3	Aüwaerter Skyliner	CH57/20CT	1984	Ex Safedrive Cs, Shenley, 1995
C908GUD	MCW Metroliner DR130/21	MCW	CH53/21FT	1986	Ex Jumboliner, Birmingham, 1995
C86NNV	Iveco-Fiat 79.14	Caetano Viana	C19F	1986	Ex Jones, Llansilin, 1993
D860LND	Renault-Dodge S56	Northern Counties	B20F	1986	Ex MTL (Fareway), 1995
D421FEH	Freight Rover Sherpa	PMT Bursley	B20F	1986	Ex Owen, Oswestry, 1992
D38TKA	Freight Rover Sherpa	Dormobile	B16F	1987	Ex Dumfries & Galloway RC, 1994
D144UJC	Freight Rover Sherpa	Made-to-Measure	B16F	1987	Ex Alpine, Llandudno, 1994
D368JUM	Volkswagen LT55	Optare City Pacer	B25F	1987	Ex Wiltax, Shanklin, 1994
F864ONR	TAZ D3200	TAZ Dubrava	C49FT	1989	Ex Aron, Northolt, 1992
H236RUX	Hestair Duple SDA1512	Duple 425	C51FT	1990	Ex Owen's, Oswestry, 1995

Previous Registrations:

A385XGG	A331UFE, 4009SC	OIB5647	A323HFP, 2086PP, A481KRT
D144UJC	D913MVU	URC158X	PRR4X, YRC194
MAB181X	PNT844X, LSV548		

Livery: Red and white or white

Two former Clwyd contracts are operated from Oswestry, route 60 to Llanarmon Duffryn Clwyd and 79, through home territory to Llanrhaeadr ym Mochnant and Llangynog. Both were former Crosville services. Typical of the vehicles to be found on the service is former Trent Leopard BRC140T though it was in Aberystwyth when photographed.
Ralph Stevens

THOMAS BROS

G Thomas, Towy Garage, Llangadog, Carmarthenshire SA19 9LU

Depots :Rhosmaen Street, Llandeilo and Towy Garage, Llangadog

DHW293K	Bristol LH6L	Eastern Coach Works	B43F	1971	Ex Bristol, 1981
GHV505N	Bristol LHS6L	Eastern Coach Works	B26F	1974	Ex London Transport, 1982
LAL746P	Leyland Leopard PSU3C/4R	Willowbrook Warrior (1988)	DP47F	1975	Ex Nottingham, 1982
KTT38P	Bristol LH6L	Eastern Coach Works	B43F	1975	Ex Devon General, 1985
KHU326P	Bristol LH6L	Eastern Coach Works	B43F	1975	Ex Bristol, 1983
TMB880R	Leyland Leopard PSU4D/2R	Duple Dominant	B47F	1976	Ex Chester, 1989
TMJ643R	Bristol LHS6L	Plaxton Supreme III	C35F	1977	Ex George, Hare Street, 1984
VDV133S	Bristol LHS6L	Plaxton Supreme III Express	C41F	1978	Ex Devon General, 1985
PRO439W	Bristol LHS6L	Plaxton Supreme IV	C33F	1978	Ex Evans, Tregaron, 1991
AEF878A	Leyland Leopard PSU3E/4R	Plaxton Viewmaster IV	C53F	1979	Ex Gower Cs, Gorseinon, 1996
NMV617W	Leyland Leopard PSU5D/5R	Plaxton Supreme IV	C55F	1981	Ex Second City Travel, Sutton Coldfield, 1993
ABW82X	Leyland Leopard PSU3F/5R	Plaxton Supreme VI Express	C53F	1982	Ex Cheney, Banbury, 1987
AEF991Y	Leyland Tiger TRCTL11/2R	Plaxton Paramount 3200 E	C53F	1983	Ex BTS, Borehamwood,
A17TBC	Leyland Tiger TRCTL11/3RH	Duple 340	C51F	1986	Ex Crosville, 1989
D631BPL	Dennis Lancet SDA525	Duple Dominant	B43F	1987	Ex Dennis demonstrator, 1988
A18TBC	DAF MB230DKVL615	Plaxton Paramount 3500 III	C49FT	1987	Ex Smith, Alcester, 1988
E212TEP	Freight Rover Sherpa	Freight Rover	M12	1988	
H16TBC	Ford Transit VE6	Zodiac	M14	1991	Ex van, 1994

Previous Registrations:

A17TBC	C69JTU	ABW82X	DFE361X, USU800	H16TBC	H407KOV
A18TBC	D129ACX	AEF878A	JTM104V, AEF667A		

Livery: Cream and green; cream, green, and red (coaches)

The close proximity of a Hutchison of Overtown Volvo B10M with Van Hool Alizée bodywork to the Thomas Bros Duple-bodied Leyland Tiger, A17TBC, and the leafless trees in Cardiff's Alexanda Gardens all point to 17th February 1996 when the Welsh Rugby team met Scotland at the National Stadium. *John Jones*

Thomas Bros still operate a fleet of four Bristol LHs and three LHSs. The veteran, having served Thomas Bros for considerably longer than it served Bristol Omnibus is DHW293K. It received some renovation before attending the Bristol Rally in 1995. *John Jones*

Plaxton Supreme VI Express bodywork is carried by Thomas Bros' ABW82X. The vehicle was new to the Lincolnshire operator Eagre Coaches and arrived with Thomas Bros through Skills of Nottingham, Holloway of Scunthorpe and Cheney of Banbury. *John Jones*

VALE OF LLANGOLLEN

T M, P R & E M Roberts, Hilbre, Well Street, Cefn Mawr, Wrexham   LL14 3YD

1	3587VT	Leyland Leopard PSU3A/2R	Northern Counties	B53F	1971	Ex NCB, Barnsley, 1985
2	467VT	Leyland Atlantean AN68/1R	Alexander AL	H45/29F	1973	Ex Strathclyde, 1983
3	7239VT	Leyland Leopard PSU3B/4R	Plaxton Elite II	C53F	1972	Ex Ellerby, Tow Law, 1985
4	3810VT	Leyland Atlantean AN68/1R	East Lancashire	H45/33F	1973	Ex Rhymney Valley, 1986
5	791VT	Leyland Leopard PSU3B/4R	Duple Dominant	C53F	1974	Ex NCB, Barnsley, 1985
6	440VT	Leyland Leopard PSU3B/4R	Plaxton Elite III	C47F	1974	Ex National Travel East, 1985
7	1260VT	Leyland Leopard PSU3B/4R	Plaxton Elite III	C47F	1974	Ex National Travel East, 1985
8	9509VT	Leyland Leopard PSU5/4R	Plaxton Elite II	C57F	1972	Ex Hollis, Queensferry, 1984
9w	2090VT	Ailsa B55-10	Alexander AV	H44/31D	1976	Ex Tayside, 1988
10	4384VT	Ailsa B55-10	Alexander AV	H44/31D	1976	Ex Tayside, 1988
11	8177VT	Ailsa B55-10	Alexander AV	H44/31D	1976	Ex Tayside, 1988
12w	1810VT	Ailsa B55-10	Alexander AV	H44/31D	1979	Ex Tayside, 1994
13w	2378VT	Ailsa B55-10	Alexander AV	H44/31D	1976	Ex Tayside, 1988
14	6400VT	Ailsa B55-10	Alexander AV	H44/31D	1977	Ex Tayside, 1994
15	6052VT	Ailsa B55-10	Alexander AV	H44/31D	1977	Ex Tayside, 1993
16	VLT483	Ailsa B55-10	Alexander AV	H44/31D	1976	Ex Tayside, 1995
	WTS267T	Ailsa B55-10	Alexander AV	H44/31D	1977	Ex Tayside, 1995
	A153HLV	Volvo B55-10 Mk III	Alexander AV	H44/37F	1984	Ex MTL (Merseybus), 1996
	A155HLV	Volvo B55-10 Mk III	Alexander AV	H44/37F	1984	Ex MTL (Merseybus), 1996
	A157HLV	Volvo B55-10 Mk III	Alexander AV	H44/37F	1984	Ex MTL (Merseybus), 1996
23	9975VT	Volvo B10M-60	Plaxton Paramount 3500 III	C55F	1988	
24	8701VT	Volvo B10M-61	Plaxton Paramount 3500 III	C53F	1989	
25	4051VT	Volvo B10M-61	Plaxton Paramount 3500 III	C55F	1988	
26	5958VT	Volvo B10M-61	Plaxton Paramount 3500 III	C55F	1988	
27	6468VT	Volvo B10M-61	Plaxton Paramount 3500 III	C55F	1988	
28	7052VT	Volvo B10M-60	Plaxton Paramount 3500 III	C53F	1989	
29	VLT280	Volvo B10M-60	Jonckheere Deauville P599	C51F	1990	Ex Budden's, Romsey, 1993
30	VLT288	Volvo B10M-60	Jonckheere Deauville P599	C51FT	1990	Ex Dace, Sutton, 1993
31	VLT293	Volvo B10M-60	Jonckheere Deauville P599	C51F	1990	Ex Budden's, Romsey, 1993
32	VLT55	Volvo B10M-60	Jonckheere Deauville P599	C51F	1990	Ex McLeans, Witney, 1994
33	VLT191	Volvo B10M-60	Jonckheere Deauville P599	C51FT	1992	
34	VLT250	Volvo B10M-60	Jonckheere Deauville P599	C51FT	1992	
35	VLT149	Volvo B10M-60	Jonckheere Deauville P599	C51FT	1992	
36	VLT177	Volvo B10M-60	Jonckheere Deauville P599	C51FT	1992	
37	L3VLT	Volvo B10M-60	Jonckheere Deauville 45	C51FT	1994	
38	L4VLT	Volvo B10M-60	Jonckheere Deauville 45	C51FT	1994	
39	L5VLT	Volvo B10M-60	Jonckheere Deauville 45	C51FT	1994	
40	L6VLT	Volvo B10M-60	Jonckheere Deauville 45	C51FT	1994	
	N2VLT	Volvo B10M-62	Jonckheere Deauville 45	C51FT	1996	
	N3VLT	Volvo B10M-62	Jonckheere Deauville 45	C51FT	1996	
		Volvo B10M-62	Jonckheere Deauville 45	C51FT	1996	
		Volvo B10M-62	Jonckheere Deauville 45	C51FT	1996	

Previous Registrations:

Livery: Sand, orange and blue

Vale of Llangollen's contract fleet, apart from the continuing arrival of Ailsa double-deck buses has not changed greatly for some time. 7239VT was new to Hearn of Harrow Weald and has retained its VT index mark for some ten years. Recently, the coach fleet has included the attractive Jonckheere Deauville coach-based on Volvo B10Ms. With many of the type now operating on the main coach duties they are a familiar sight throughout Britain, several in Cosmos' white & red livery. *John Jones*

The first pair of Ailsa-assembled Volvo buses arrived from Tayside in 1988, until then Leyland Atlanteans were the preferred choice for double-deckers. Now carrying 4384VT, NSP312R was one of this first pair, though regrettably its twin was burnt out in a fire at Cefn Mawr. *John Jones*

VOEL COACHES

JS, B, WM & M Kerfoot-Davies, Penisa Filling Station, Longacres Road, Dyserth, Denbighshire LL18 6BP

JC9736	Guy Wolf NLW	Barnard	B21F	1949	Ex Hollis, Queensferry, 1982
TGX759M	Daimler Fleetline CRL6	Park Royal	H44/28D	1973	Ex Crown Coaches, Bristol, 1990
VRP60S	Bristol VRT/SL3/6LXB	Alexander AL	H45/27D	1977	Ex Northampton, 1992
VVV63S	Bristol VRT/SL3/6LXB	Alexander AL	H45/27D	1977	Ex Northampton, 1992
UUX845S	Bedford YMT	Plaxton Supreme III Express	C53F	1978	Ex Owen's, Oswestry, 1987
HFM962T	Volvo B58-56	Plaxton Supreme III	C53F	1978	Ex Hanmer, Southsea, 1979
GPA611V	Ford R1114	Duple Dominant II	C53F	1980	Ex Hodge, Sandhurst, 1984
GPA613V	Ford R1114	Duple Dominant II	C53F	1980	Ex Hodge, Sandhurst, 1984
GPA614V	Ford R1114	Duple Dominant II	C53F	1980	Ex Hodge, Sandhurst, 1984
7934VC	Volvo B58-61	Plaxton Supreme IV	C57F	1980	Ex Terry Shaw, Barnsley, 1983
776VC	Volvo B10M-61	Caetano Alpha	C53F	1981	
VWX366X	Volvo B10M-61	Plaxton Supreme V	C51F	1982	Ex Wallace Arnold, 1982
601MMA	Volvo B10M-61	Van Hool Alizée	C48FT	1984	Ex Eagles & Crawford, Mold, 1988
6499VC	Volvo B10M-61	Van Hool Alizée	C50FT	1984	
7488VC	Volvo B10M-61	Van Hool Alizée	C50FT	1984	
9155VC	Van Hool T815	Van Hool Alizée	C53F	1984	
8214VC	Volvo B10M-61	Plaxton Paramount 3500 II	C53F	1985	Ex Frames Rickards, Brentford, 1991
G415YAY	Dennis Javelin 12SDA1907	Duple 320	C57F	1990	
1760VC	Dennis Javelin 12SDA1907	Duple 320	C57F	1990	
8868VC	Scania K112CRB	Plaxton Paramount 3500 III	C49FT	1990	Ex Westerham Coaches, 1994
M2OVC	Scania K113CRB	Van Hool Alizée	C53FT	1995	
M3OVC	Scania K113CRB	Van Hool Alizée	C53FT	1995	

Previous Registrations:

601MMA	A204VCA, 984FJB	7488VC	From new		8868VC	G998HKW
776VC	YFM289W	7934VC	HKY614W		9155VC	A541XDM
1760VC	G425YAY	8214VC	B533BML		JC9736	From new
6499VC	From new					

Livery: Two-tone orange and white

At first sight one may think this to be an Ailsa, but it is one of thirty-six Bristol VRTs built for Northampton in 1977-78. A further 71 single-door examples were supplied to Cardiff between 1978 and 1980. VRP60S is now with Voel Coaches of Dyserth, near Prestatyn.
John Jones

WILLIAMS ♦ BALA

Williams (Bala) Ltd, Bodolwyn Garage, Brenig Street, Bala, Gwynedd, LL23 7AH

PVS43R	Bedford VAS5	Plaxton Supreme III	C29F	1977	Ex Formby Coaches, 1988
DOA714V	Bedford YMT	Plaxton Supreme IV	C53F	1979	Ex Hammond Cs, Stoney Stanton, 1994
TDM769V	Leyland Leopard PSU3F/4R	Duple Dominant II	C53F	1980	Ex Formby Coaches, 1991
NDW140X	Leyland Tiger TRCTL11/2R	Plaxton Supreme V Express	C53F	1982	Ex Formby Coaches, 1988
NMA746Y	Mercedes-Benz L508D	Devon Conversions	C19F	1983	Ex Formby Coaches, 1988
HEY78Y	Ford R1114	Plaxton Paramount 3200	C53F	1983	Ex KMP, Llanberis, 1989
DIW3778	Leyland Tiger TRCTL11/3R	Plaxton Paramount 3500	C49FT	1983	Ex Dorking Coaches, 1994
WWE222Y	Leyland Tiger TRCTL11/3R	Plaxton Paramount 3500	C50F	1983	Ex Dorking Coaches, 1994
A712NGS	Ford Transit	Chassis Developments	M12	1983	Ex Dorking Coaches, 1994
A715XSC	Mercedes-Benz LP813	Imperial	C29F	1984	Ex Sproat, Bouth, 1992
FIL4135	Leyland Tiger TRCTL11/3R	Plaxton Paramount 3500 II	C49FT	1985	Ex Travelmate, Wareham, 1995
E795CCA	Mercedes-Benz 709D	PMT	C25F	1988	Ex Bryn Melyn, Llangollen, 1993

Previous Registrations:

DIW3778	BAJ634Y	FIL4135	B406CMC	WWE222Y	GRH1Y, RHE194

Livery: White and red

The Williams - Bala fleet had connections with Formby Coaches on Merseyside until a change of ownership in 1994 though four vehicles from that operator remain. One of these, NDW140X was new to Hill's of Tredegar and features a Plaxton Supreme V body on an 11-metre Leyland Tiger chassis. The revised front grille is of interest. *Ralph Stevens*

Williams of Brecon celebrated 40 years of business in 1995. Demonstrating how things have changed in that time is their latest purchase, N5DMW. This MAN 10.180 chassis continues a preference for MAN or Daimler-Benz powered vehicles. The new arrival was entered in the 1996 British Coach Rally at Brighton and returned with the Salvador Caetano Trophy for the best Caetano-bodied vehicle. The opportunity was taken in 1993 to acquire some relatively youthful Kässbohrer Setra coaches, HEU350, the youngest of the three is seen outside the depot in Brecon. *David Donati*

WILLIAMS

Williams Motors (Cwmdu) Ltd, Rich Way, The Watton, Brecon, Powys, LD3 7EA.

Depots :Rich Way, Brecon; Canal Road, Brecon and Crescent Garage, Cwmdu

TPJ270S	Bedford YMT	Plaxton Supreme III	C53F	1977	Ex Hardings, Betchworth, 1995
BUS960S	Bedford VAS5	Duple Dominant	C29F	1978	Ex Marks, Plymouth, 1996
CRW510T	Bedford YMT	Plaxton Supreme IV	C53F	1978	Ex Evans, Tregaron, 1995
NAB848T	Bedford YLQ	Plaxton Supreme IV	C45F	1979	Ex Yarranton, Eardiston, 1984
YAD739X	Bedford YMT	Caetano Alpha	C49F	1981	Ex Murgatroyd, Thruscross, 1983
GFO775X	Bedford YMQ	Duple Dominant II	C45F	1981	
KFO181Y	Bedford CFL	Robin Hood	M12	1982	
299DMW	Mercedes-Benz 0303/15R	Mercedes-Benz	C49F	1982	Ex Redwing, Camberwell, 1987
226DMW	Mercedes-Benz 0303/15RHP	Mercedes-Benz	C49F	1982	Ex Redwing, Camberwell, 1987
GWO1L	Mercedes Benz 0303/15R	Mercedes Benz	C51FT	1983	Ex Luckett, Fareham, 1992
5583HA	Mercedes-Benz 0303/15R	Jonckheere Jubilee P50	C51FT	1983	Ex Berryhurst, Vauxhall, 1987
A417CRM	Mercedes-Benz 307D	Reeve Burgess	M12	1983	Ex Woods, Treforest, 1985
A733RCA	Mercedes-Benz 608D	MB/Williams	C21F	1983	
WSU259	Kässbohrer Setra S215HD	Kässbohrer Tornado	C53F	1986	Ex Landtourers, Farnham, 1993
YSU903	Kässbohrer Setra S215HD	Kässbohrer Tornado	C53F	1986	Ex Landtourers, Farnham, 1993
HEU350	Kassbohrer Setra S215HD	Kassbohrer Tornado	C49FT	1986	Ex Priory, Gosport, 1992
IIL8520	Mercedes-Benz 609D	Reeve Burgess	C19F	1987	
MIB552	DAF MB230LB615	Caetano Algarve	C49FT	1988	Ex The King's Ferry, 1993
E222WMB	Mercedes-Benz 307D	Advanced Vehicle Bodies	M12	1987	Ex Safeway, Batley, 1996
F700JNU	Ford Transit VE6	Ford	M14	1989	Ex Cox's Taxi Services, Belper, 1994
F483OCN	Mercedes-Benz 408D	G & M Coachworks	M16	1989	Ex Marks, Plymouth, 1996
G818UPX	Mercedes-Benz 308D	Devon Conversions	M12	19	Ex Lewis, Llanrhystyd, 1994
IIL8518	DAF SB3000DKV	Caetano Algarve	C51FT	1990	
IIL8519	DAF SB3000DKV	Caetano Algarve	C51FT	1990	
IIL8522	Sanos S315.21	FAP Charisma	C49FT	1990	Ex Chartercoach, Great Oakley, 1992
H160NBF	Ford Transit VE6	Premier	M8	1991	Ex van, 1994
IIL8521	Toyota Coaster HDB30R	Caetano Optimo II	C21F	1991	Ex Taylor's, Sutton Scotney, 1996
M5JLW	MAN 18.370HOCLR	Caetano Algarve II	C49FT	1995	
N5DMW	MAN 11.190HOCLR	Caetano Algarve II	C35F	1996	

Previous Registrations:

226DMW	PUL94Y, ALJ664A	IIL8521	J234HVK
299DMW	PUL80Y, ALJ587A	IIL8522	G968CNO
5583HA	A130SNH	MIB552	E179KNH
GWO1L	PUL93Y ALJ805A	NBZ1844	-
HEU350	D620WPJ	WSU259	C209UPC
IIL8518	G149TVJ	YAD739X	VYG694X, DMW307
IIL8519	G150TVJ	YSU903	C210UPC, YSU904
IIL8520	D449BFO		

Livery: Cream, orange and brown

WILLIAMS DEINIOLEN

I W & E Williams (Ieuan Williams Coaches), Glanffrwd, Gallt-y-Foel, Deiniolen, Gwynedd, LL55 3HH

Depot :Glanffrwd, Gallt-y-Foel; Griffiths Crossing Industrial Estate, Caernarfon

BJV99L	Daimler Fleetline CRG6LX	Roe	H45/29D	1973	Ex Grimsby-Cleethorpes, 1990
KCG614L	Leyland National 1151/1R/0402		B49F	1973	Ex Eastern National, 1987
NPK234R	Leyland National 10351A/1R		B41F	1976	Ex London Country NW, 1990
YBW602R	Bristol VRT/SL3/6LXB	Eastern Coach Works	H43/31F	1976	Ex South Midland, 1988
PKY416R	Bedford YLQ	Plaxton Supreme III	C45F	1977	Ex Balby Carr School, 1995
DWY148T	Bristol VRT/SL3/6LXB	Eastern Coach Works	H43/31F	1979	Ex Tees & District, 1994
K542OGA	Mercedes-Benz 811D	Dormobile Routemaker	B33F	1992	
N523DCC	Mercedes-Benz 811D	Wright Nim-Bus	B31F	1995	

Livery: Red, white and blue

T WILLIAMS & SONS

J S Williams, Clarke Street, Ponciau, Wrexham LL14 1RT

Depot :Aberderfyn, Ponciau

GFM333T	Bedford YLQ	Duple Dominant II	C45F	1978	
SFM10V	DAF MB200DKTL550	Plaxton Supreme IV	C53F	1980	Ex Hanmer, Southsea, 1985
UKH170W	Bedford YMT	Plaxton Bustler	B55F	1981	Ex Plaxton demonstrator, 1981
A800SMB	Bedford YNT	Duple Dominant	B53F	1983	
UAM829	Volvo B10M-61	Jonckheere Jubilee P50	C53FT	1983	Ex Vale of Llangollen, 1993

Previous Registrations:
UAM829   NVV553Y, 8701VT, VLT55

Livery: Blue and cream (buses); blue and white (coaches)

Ieuan Williams of Deiniolen added this former Tees & District Bristol VR to the fleet shortly after the last Welsh Bus Handbook was printed. University of Wales, Bangor, provides the backdrop as it approaches Y Cloc at the end of the run from Llanberis. *John Jones*

T Williams & Son no longer operate bus services though they retain their two bus-bodied Bedfords for use on school contracts. In addition, the coach fleet contains eighteen-year-old Bedford YLQ GFM333T seen here with a Duple Dominant II body. *John Jones*

Index to Vehicles

Reg	Operator	Reg	Operator	Reg	Operator	Reg	Operator
7CCH	K M P	3338DD	Davies Bros	A36VDE	Davies Bros	AJA421L	Silcox
20KB43	Davies Bros	3475DD	Davies Bros	A44KLF	James Brothers	AKK172T	Carreglefn Cs
20KB79	Davies Bros	3587VT	Vale of Llangollen	A49VDE	Davies Bros	AKM433K	Davies Bros
34BCG	Clynnog & Trefor	3810VT	Vale of Llangollen	A71VTX	Davies Bros	AKW965T	Longs
102UTF	Goodsir	4051VT	Vale of Llangollen	A101CVN	Devaway	ANA91Y	Tanat Valley
108BDL	T S Lewis	4384VT	Vale of Llangollen	A102CVN	Devaway	ANY586T	Oare's of Holywell
109CUF	Silcox	4858DW	Gwyn Williams	A103CVN	Devaway	APH523T	Cross Gates Cs
151WYB	M & H Travel	5182PO	P & O Lloyd	A104CVN	Devaway	ATA556L	Ellis Travel
226DMW	Williams, Cwmdu	5373PO	P & O Lloyd	A105CVN	Devaway	ATH180T	Meyers
241KRO	Ellis Travel	538OHU	Silcox	A106CVN	Devaway	ATV182T	Celtic
250DBX	Midway Motors	5519DD	Davies Bros	A115UDE	Davies Bros	AUJ746T	James Brothers
264ACA	Eagles & Crawford	5583HA	Williams, Cwmdu	A153HLV	Vale of Llangollen	AYG849S	Express Motors
297EYR	Goodsir	5652MT	Gwyn Williams	A156HLV	Vale of Llangollen	B10MMJ	Jones International
299DMW	Williams, Cwmdu	5889VC	W E Jones & Son	A157HLV	Vale of Llangollen	B40BCA	Clwydian Tours
341TJ	Lewis Y Llan	5958VT	Vale of Llangollen	A178SHD	Cross Gates Cs	B44MRF	Berwyn
349LVO	Celtic	6052VT	Vale of Llangollen	A200PCJ	Edward Bros	B89CDS	Nefyn Coaches
367ARV	Arvonia	6400VT	Vale of Llangollen	A233GNR	Lewis Whitland	B101KPF	Prestatyn Cs
428EJB	Empire Goldstar	6468VT	Vale of Llangollen	A343ASF	Berwyn	B176WYV	Empire Goldstar
440VT	Vale of Llangollen	6499VC	Voel Coaches	A345VEP	Jones Llanfaethlu	B183WYV	Empire Goldstar
467VT	Vale of Llangollen	6690DD	Davies Bros	A373XTG	Browns of Builth	B191BLG	Crosville
5210DD	Davies Bros	6697RU	K M P	A385XGG	Tanat Valley	B192BLG	Crosville
521WDE	Jones of Login	6709PO	P & O Lloyd	A417CRM	Williams, Cwmdu	B193BLG	Crosville
526FDE	Jones of Login	6738UN	James Brothers	A419FSA	G H A Coaches	B194BLG	Crosville
526NDE	Edward Bros	7052VT	Vale of Llangollen	A419XHL	Fisher	B196BLG	Crosville
529FN	Cross Gates Cs	7074DK	Cross Gates Cs	A511LPP	Browns of Builth	B218JPH	W E Jones & Son
546FJB	Empire Goldstar	7239VT	Vale of Llangollen	A594GWM	Selwyn Hughes	B258AMG	Nefyn Coaches
572RKJ	Owen's	7289DD	Davies Bros	A606UGD	Celtic	B440VOW	Ellis Travel
600DBX	T S Lewis	7488VC	Voel Coaches	A609XFM	Great Orme Tours	B511TFO	Edward Bros
600KPU	T S Lewis	7660DD	Davies Bros	A647GLD	Fisher	B559KRY	Alpine
601MMA	Voel Coaches	7934VC	Voel Coaches	A698AWB	George Edwards	B567NCC	Alpine
604JPU	Express Motors	8098DD	Davies Bros	A712NGS	Williams - Bala	B590HEJ	Mid Wales Motorways
607VYC	Acton Coaches	8124DD	Davies Bros	A715XSC	Williams - Bala	B620OJC	Alpine
610LYB	Empire Goldstar	8177VT	Vale of Llangollen	A733RCA	Williams, Cwmdu	B624DEV	Selwyn Hughes
668VDE	Edward Bros	8214VC	Voel Coaches	A734JAY	Edward Bros	B634BEP	Gwyn Williams
691DDE	Alpine	8443PH	Express Motors	A741DCN	W E Jones & Son	B665OFP	Ffoshelig
730MMJ	Jones International	8701VT	Vale of Llangollen	A800SMB	T Williams & Son	B679EWE	Phillips
772URB	K M P	8853DD	Davies Bros	A801LEY	Alpine	B804TCJ	Browns of Builth
776VC	Voel Coaches	8868VC	Voel Coaches	A80RGE	Express Motors	B955BSU	Browns of Builth
779HCY	T S Lewis	9155VC	Voel Coaches	A829JEY	Nefyn Coaches	B991UPS	Oare's of Holywell
791VT	Vale of Llangollen	9195PU	Silcox	A860KFP	D & G Coaches	BAZ7378	Goodsir
798EYG	Goodsir	9284UN	Clwydian Tours	A945MDH	Browns of Builth	BBB544V	Celtic
804SHW	Silcox	9509VT	Vale of Llangollen	A946MDH	Browns of Builth	BBM62A	E Jones & Son
817FKH	Silcox	9616DD	Davies Bros	AAZ9091	M & H Travel	BBR736S	Edward Bros
834TDE	Jones of Login	9975VT	Vale of Llangollen	AAZ9102	Berwyn	BBR738S	Richard Bros
846MBF	Clwydian Tours	A2ARV	Arvonia	ABN772V	Longs	BBX190V	Richard Bros
875EPX	Nefyn Coaches	A2NPT	Nefyn Coaches	ABR778S	Tanat Valley	BBX915V	Silcox
891VDE	Edward Bros	A2WLS	Silcox	ABV166R	Phillips	BCJ680V	Berwyn
947JWD	Fisher	A3WLS	Silcox	ABW82X	Thomas Bros	BCJ710B	Jones International
951SAU	Alpine	A4WLS	Silcox	ACA189S	Rogers	BCS867T	P & O Lloyd
963CDE	Jones of Login	A5NPT	Berwyn	ACA666A	M & H Travel	BDE140V	Silcox
984FJB	Empire Goldstar	A5WLS	Silcox	ACA912S	Clwydian Tours	BDE143V	Silcox
997EAY	Carreglefn Cs	A6WLS	Silcox	ADE612V	Richard Bros	BDE792V	Jones of Login
1260VT	Vale of Llangollen	A7KMP	K M P	ADN51V	Longs	BEC819S	Cross Gates Cs
164EWN	James Brothers	A7ORJ	Jones Llanfaethlu	ADU327X	Davies Bros	BEN271V	Stafford's
1760VC	Voel Coaches	A7WLS	Silcox	AEC732S	W E Jones & Son	BEP964V	K M P
1810VT	Vale of Llangollen	A8WLS	Silcox	AEF221Y	Crosville	BEP969V	K M P
1862HX	Empire Goldstar	A9WLS	Silcox	AEF222Y	Crosville	BEU809V	Longs
1885FM	Midway Motors	A11WLS	Silcox	AEF224Y	Crosville	BEY7W	Purple
1923DD	Davies Bros	A12WLS	Silcox	AEF229Y	Crosville	BFJ209T	Clynnog & Trefor
2090VT	Vale of Llangollen	A14WLS	Silcox	AEF878A	Thomas Bros	BFP248Y	John's Travel
2358DD	Davies Bros	A15WLS	Silcox	AEF991Y	Thomas Bros	BHO57R	Goodsir
2378VT	Vale of Llangollen	A16WLS	Silcox	AEY220	Jones Llanfaethlu	BJV99L	Williams Deiniolen
2405DD	Davies Bros.	A17TBC	Thomas Bros	AEY365	Jones Llanfaethlu	BMA520W	Crosville
2934MM	Midway Motors	A18TBC	Thomas Bros	AHU512V	Eagles & Crawford	BMA521W	Crosville
329UWL	James Brothers	A36DTV	Fisher	AJA418L	Silcox	BMA522W	Crosville

The North & West Wales Bus Handbook

Now happily replaced in its role as senior member of the road fleet, YHP760J, a mere 25 years old, is a positive youth compared with reinstated JC8344 portrayed on page 53. Neither can hold a candle to the funicular tram cars recently refurbished. *John Jones*

BMA524W	Crosville	C258UAJ	Crosville	CEJ939Y	Llithfaen Motors	D81VCC	Crosville
BNE765N	Silver Star	C284AOR	Pied Bull	CFF25Y	James Brothers	D82VCC	Crosville
BNT667T	Bryn Melyn	C302SPL	Crosville	CFO700V	Browns of Builth	D83VCC	Crosville
BPT927S	Alpine	C303SPL	Crosville	CGA199X	Mid Wales Motorways	D84VCC	Crosville
BPT928S	Alpine	C304SPL	Crosville	CIB7866	G H A Coaches	D85VCC	Crosville
BRC140T	Tanat Valley	C306SPL	Crosville	CKC301L	Empire Goldstar	D86VCC	Crosville
BRC838T	Alpine	C307SPL	Crosville	CKC304L	Empire Goldstar	D87VCC	Crosville
BRC840T	Alpine	C315DVU	Pied Bull	CKC327L	Empire Goldstar	D88VCC	Crosville
BTO291T	Clynnog & Trefor	C324LDT	D & G Coaches	CKC336L	Empire Goldstar	D89VCC	Crosville
BTU364S	G H A Coaches	C327PEW	Express Motors	CKC343L	Empire Goldstar	D90VCC	Crosville
BTU368S	Crosville	C334GTH	Richard Bros	CKC928X	Devaway	D91VCC	Crosville
BTX42V	Alpine	C410WCJ	Browns of Builth	CNP316B	Jones Llanfaethlu	D92VCC	Crosville
BUR712S	Silcox	C433HHL	Prestatyn Cs	CPT737S	Alpine	D94VCC	Crosville
BUS960S	Williams, Cwmdu	C441BHY	Express Motors	CRW510T	Williams, Cwmdu	D96VCC	Crosville
BUX204L	Clwydian Tours	C454BHY	Express Motors	CUN669L	Pied Bull	D103UJC	John's Travel
BVJ771V	Lewis Y Llan	C458BHY	Summerdale	CUT402T	Cross Gates Cs	D104TFT	Padarn
BVJ780V	Lewis Y Llan	C472LKU	George Edwards	CWG707V	Silcox	D109WCC	Clynnog & Trefor
BVR87T	K M P	C483TAY	Acton Coaches	CWG712V	Silcox	D110CRE	Browns of Builth
BVU917N	Jones Llanfaethlu	C486TPG	Celtic	CWG748V	Tanat Valley	D113XVX	Mid Wales Motorways
BWJ68T	G H A Coaches	C513TJF	Arvonia	CWG759V	Silcox	D114WCC	Clynnog & Trefor
BWK8T	Gwyn Williams	C514DND	Fisher	CYG154H	Empire Goldstar	D128NON	Clynnog & Trefor
BXI637	Jones International	C523BFB	Empire Goldstar	D28KAX	Sel's	D141LTA	Davies Bros
C27BPR	Fisher	C543HCA	Clwydian Tours	D30BVV	Sel's	D141NON	Longs
C63JTU	Crosville	C745TJF	James Brothers	D30KAX	Sel's	D142NON	Clynnog & Trefor
C83GTH	Gwyn Williams	C826CBU	Ffoshelig	D30TKA	Phillips	D143HML	Nefyn Coaches
C86NNV	Tanat Valley	C830XCJ	Phillips	D31RWC	Crosville	D143WCC	Eagles & Crawford
C167XFO	Browns of Builth	C900JGA	Padarn	D32RWC	Crosville	D144UJC	Tanat Valley
C208GTU	Crosville	C908GUD	Tanat Valley	D38TKA	Tanat Valley	D147NON	Gwyn Williams
C209GTU	Crosville	CBM293T	Bryn Melyn	D40OTH	Nefyn Coaches	D153VRP	Crosville
C210GTU	Crosville	CCC596	Alpine	D44AVJ	Richard Bros	D154LTA	D & G Coaches
C211GTU	Crosville	CCP433V	Clynnog & Trefor	D52MBO	Gwyn Williams	D154VRP	Crosville
C212GTU	Crosville	CEF230Y	Crosville	D79VCC	Crosville	D158VRP	Arvonia
C248SPC	Crosville	CEF232Y	Crosville	D80VCC	Crosville	D159LTA	Davies Bros

Reg	Operator	Reg	Operator	Reg	Operator	Reg	Operator
D163NCY	Longs	D914BFO	Browns of Builth	E238MBX	Ffoshelig	F133UDE	Richard Bros
D165KDN	Rogers	D915BFO	Browns of Builth	E255PEL	Edward Bros	F201JGH	Sel's
D165NON	Stafford's	D920PGB	Midway Motors	E299OMG	Crosville	F207EFK	Midway Motors
D166VRP	Jones Llanfaethlu	D946KBU	Gwyn Williams	E302HHP	K M P	F209PNR	Selwyn Hughes
D167VRP	Crosville	D948UDY	G H A Coaches	E312XGB	G H A Coaches	F210DCC	Crosville
D169LTA	Davies Bros	D955UDY	Jones Llanfaethlu	E316ACC	Nefyn Coaches	F211DCC	Crosville
D169VRP	Crosville	D956UDY	Crosville	E328OMG	Crosville	F212DCC	Crosville
D170VRP	Crosville	D958UDY	Crosville	E329EVH	Browns of Builth	F213DCC	Crosville
D171VRP	Crosville	D958WJH	Gwyn Williams	E330OMG	James Brothers	F214DCC	Crosville
D172VRP	Crosville	D959UDY	Crosville	E333MDE	Edward Bros	F215DCC	Crosville
D173VRP	Crosville	D960UDY	Crosville	E333NBX	Gwyn Williams	F216DCC	Crosville
D174VRP	Crosville	D962UDY	Crosville	E348UOH	Longs	F217DCC	Crosville
D175VRP	Crosville	D963UDY	Crosville	E370ECJ	George Edwards	F218DCC	Crosville
D182VRP	Crosville	D965UDY	Crosville	E442YAO	Midway Motors	F219DCC	Crosville
D188VRP	Crosville	D966UDY	Crosville	E522TOV	Sel's	F220DCC	Crosville
D189VRP	Crosville	D967UDY	Crosville	E566JFR	Express Motors	F221DCC	Crosville
D191VRP	Crosville	D968UDY	Crosville	E605XWB	Mid Wales Motorways	F222DCC	Crosville
D211GLJ	Silver Star	D982OEJ	Richard Bros	E634YWL	Gwyn Williams	F223DCC	Crosville
D219GLJ	Berwyn	D983OEJ	Richard Bros	E661KCX	Alpine	F228BAX	Prestatyn Cs
D243OOJ	Longs	D98VCC	Crosville	E663KCX	Alpine	F242VBX	Gwyn Williams
D243PAW	Selwyn Hughes	D99VCC	Crosville	E669ECJ	Gwyn Williams	F258DKG	M & H Travel
D257WEY	Alpine	DAD254T	Cerbydau Cenarth	E677LDE	Edward Bros	F317VVC	Caelloi
D258HFX	Fisher	DAY1T	Express Motors	E710GNH	Gwynfor Cs	F334FWW	Richard Bros
D350KVA	Davies Bros	DBX548W	G H A Coaches	E710WNE	Oare's of Holywell	F345ONO	Oare's of Holywell
D368JUM	Tanat Valley	DBX555W	Browns of Builth	E712UHB	Owen's	F356TSX	Express Motors
D372UVL	James Brothers	DCA525X	Crosville	E716BDM	Lewis Whitland	F363MUT	Eagles & Crawford
D387SGS	Gwyn Williams	DCA527X	Crosville	E728DSO	Mid Wales Motorways	F368RPO	Ellis Travel
D401SGS	Davies Bros	DCA528X	Crosville	E737EVJ	Browns of Builth	F383MUT	Edward Bros
D416BCJ	Browns of Builth	DCA529X	Crosville	E753JAY	James Brothers	F414KHR	Devaway
D421FEH	Tanat Valley	DCA530X	Crosville	E756HJF	Eagles & Crawford	F418DAX	Oare's of Holywell
D433UHC	Crosville	DCA532X	Crosville	E788MDE	Richard Bros	F424EJC	Crosville
D434BCJ	Rogers	DCA533X	Crosville	E795CCA	Williams - Bala	F425EJC	Crosville
D434UHC	Crosville	DCA534X	Crosville	E855FVJ	T S Lewis	F426EJC	Crosville
D435UHC	Crosville	DFB233W	Owen's	E885MYP	Edward Bros	F426ENB	James Brothers
D436UHC	Crosville	DHW293K	Thomas Bros	E910UNW	Caelloi	F427AWD	Meyers
D437UHC	Crosville	DIW3778	Williams - Bala	E911UNW	Silver Star	F427EJC	Crosville
D438UHC	Crosville	DJH731F	T S Lewis	E967PME	Crosville	F428EJC	Crosville
D439UHC	Crosville	DNT465T	Selwyn Hughes	E968PME	Crosville	F480SBX	Longs
D440UHC	Crosville	DOA714V	Williams - Bala	E976LBK	Davies Bros	F481WFA	Meyers
D441UHC	Crosville	DPB777T	T S Lewis	EAA829W	Browns of Builth	F483OCN	Williams, Cwmdu
D442UHC	Crosville	DSU772	Eagles & Crawford	ECS884V	Alpine	F550DCY	Gwyn Williams
D443UHC	Crosville	DTT496T	Richard Bros	ECT912	Jones Llanfaethlu	F566ABV	Richard Bros
D444UHC	Crosville	DVR301T	W E Jones & Son	EDE38R	Midway Motors	F567ABV	Edward Bros
D445UHC	Crosville	DWY148T	Williams Deiniolen	EDT917V	K M P	F580OOU	Silcox
D446UHC	Crosville	E33EVW	Crosville	EGR704S	Browns of Builth	F585OOU	Silcox
D458CKV	Gwyn Williams	E34EVW	Crosville	EHW294W	Silcox	F595USG	Fisher
D506MJA	Sel's	E35EVW	Crosville	EJC412X	Clynnog & Trefor	F602HEC	James Brothers
D509MJA	Llithfaen Motors	E36EVW	Crosville	EMB369S	Express Motors	F612RBX	Davies Bros
D512NDA	G H A Coaches	E36RBO	Richard Bros	ERU108V	Davies Bros	F700JNU	Williams, Cwmdu
D543HNW	K D Coach Hire	E37EVW	Crosville	ERU390V	Davies Bros	F701ECC	Crosville
D564HNW	Berwyn	E76PUH	Browns of Builth	ESU294	Clynnog & Trefor	F701KMA	Crosville
D570EWS	Edward Bros	E77LRN	Gwynfor Cs	EUM891T	Devaway	F702ECC	Crosville
D574VBV	Devaway	E98DMA	E Jones Passenger	EUM893T	Alpine	F702KMA	Crosville
D580VBV	Devaway	E108OUH	G H A Coaches	EUM894T	Devaway	F704KMA	Crosville
D613WEY	Carreglefn Cs	E112RAX	G H A Coaches	EXI1726	Express Motors	F721ENE	Davies Bros
D614GDU	Browns of Builth	E121RAX	G H A Coaches	EXI2455	Express Motors	F721KCA	Clwydian Tours
D621SJX	Summerdale	E123RAX	Fisher	EXI790	Express Motors	F726ENE	Davies Bros
D631BPL	Thomas Bros	E147TBO	Browns of Builth	F21TMP	James Brothers	F747SBX	Cerbydau Cenarth
D642DRT	George Edwards	E148TBO	Browns of Builth	F21YBO	T S Lewis	F757WSC	K D Coach Hire
D659WEY	Nefyn Coaches	E149TBO	Browns of Builth	F42DJC	Alpine	F770SBX	Gwyn Williams
D700STU	Clwydian Tours	E150RNY	G H A Coaches	F43DJC	Alpine	F854YJX	Arvonia
D722JUB	Carreglefn Cs	E178TWO	Meyers	F66FKW	Crosville	F864ONR	Tanat Valley
D761PTU	Phillips	E180TWO	Acton Coaches	F67FKW	Crosville	F865DAC	Silcox
D775RBU	K D Coach Hire	E187DBB	Edward Bros	F68FKW	Crosville	F866TNH	Lewis Whitland
D777JUB	G H A Coaches	E209KCK	Davies Bros	F69FKW	Crosville	F876RDE	Richard Bros
D810KWT	Jones Llanfaethlu	E212PWY	Devaway	F70FKW	Crosville	F888CRN	Gwynfor Cs
D826KBO	Oare's of Holywell	E212TEP	Thomas Bros	F113UBX	Davies Bros	F904NBB	Oare's of Holywell
D854CKV	Silcox	E213PWY	Devaway	F114UBX	Davies Bros	F916TTP	Alpine
D860LND	Tanat Valley	E216PWY	Devaway	F130DMB	Clwydian Tours	F947CUA	Jones Llanfaethlu
D900STU	Purple	E222WMB	Williams, Cwmdu	F130TRU	Edward Bros	F951CUA	P & O Lloyd

Mid Wales Motorways contributes to the executive Eurolines network with two Volvo coaches and a Leyland Tiger. These carry the Eurolines livery though M874UEJ was photographed at Llandyssul between Lampeter and Newcastle Emlyn. *John Jones*

F977DEY	Caelloi	G112JBO	George Edwards	G241GCC	Crosville	GBX484W	Jones of Login
FAZ3193	Crosville	G121GOJ	Ellis Travel	G242GCC	Crosville	GCC487Y	Alpine
FAZ3194	Crosville	G137TNU	Owen's	G243GCC	Crosville	GCC572	Carreglefn Cs
FAZ5181	Crosville	G142JCC	Alpine	G255PGN	Sel's	GCY751N	Alpine
FBX560W	Llithfaen Motors	G144RCA	Clwydian Tours	G256EHD	George Edwards	GDE148X	Jones of Login
FBX561W	E Jones Passenger	G151FJC	Crosville	G258EHD	Eagles & Crawford	GDE371W	Davies Bros
FBZ1473	M & H Travel	G152FJC	Crosville	G261EHD	George Edwards	GDZ886	Gwyn Williams
FCY296W	Celtic	G160YRE	Crosville	G278HDW	Pied Bull	GEY124	Carreglefn Cs
FCY297W	Celtic	G161YRE	Crosville	G300LEP	Gwyn Williams	GEY371	Carreglefn Cs
FDZ4166	Prestatyn Cs	G162YRE	Crosville	G304YBX	Davies Bros	GEY389Y	Purple
FEK1F	Davies Bros	G163YRE	Crosville	G358FOP	Padarn	GFJ662N	Jones Llanfaethlu
FFP200V	Midway Motors	G169FJC	Crosville	G415YAY	Voel Coaches	GFM333T	T Williams & Son
FFW508T	Richard Bros	G170FJC	Crosville	G432YAY	G H A Coaches	GFO775X	Williams, Cwmdu
FIL3825	Oare's of Holywell	G171FJC	Crosville	G464VPG	Mid Wales Motorways	GGE163T	Express Motors
FIL4135	Williams - Bala	G172FJC	Crosville	G500LWU	Caelloi	GHV505N	Thomas Bros
FIL4161	Empire Goldstar	G173FJC	Crosville	G500XBX	Gwyn Williams	GIL2987	Longs
FIL7131	Davies Bros	G174FJC	Crosville	G555HTH	Gwyn Williams	GIL3276	Midway Motors
FIW578	T S Lewis	G175FJC	Crosville	G609JET	Express Motors	GIL4128	Longs
FNE516Y	Cerbydau Cenarth	G176FJC	Crosville	G744YDE	Jones of Login	GIL4527	Longs
FOD941Y	Caelloi	G177FJC	Crosville	G761HJC	Alpine	GIL9489	Oare's of Holywell
FSU106	Clynnog & Trefor	G216EOA	M & H Travel	G762HJC	Alpine	GKK157V	Davies Bros
FSU508	Stratos Travel	G219EOA	Longs	G767RVJ	Browns of Builth	GKK158V	Davies Bros
FTU376T	Alpine	G222EOA	Express Motors	G799RNC	Browns of Builth	GMB382T	Express Motors
FTU378T	Crosville	G229FJC	Crosville	G818UPX	Williams, Cwmdu	GMB391T	T S Lewis
FUY812J	Rogers	G230FJC	Crosville	G837LWR	Richard Bros	GMB648T	Crosville
FWB494V	Gwynfor Cs	G232FJC	Crosville	G838FTX	Owen's	GMB649T	Express Motors
FYA201T	Browns of Builth	G233FJC	Crosville	G843HRN	Empire Goldstar	GMB660T	Crosville
G35HDW	Longs	G234FJC	Crosville	G848VBX	Gwyn Williams	GMB664T	Crosville
G36BBX	Davies Bros	G235FJC	Crosville	G869YBX	Cerbydau Cenarth	GMS305S	Lewis Whitland
G38YHJ	Crosville	G236FJC	Crosville	G873YDU	Fisher	GNF13V	Silcox
G39YHJ	Crosville	G237FJC	Crosville	G888HCY	Gwyn Williams	GNL839N	Silcox
G40YHJ	Crosville	G238FJC	Crosville	G978KJX	Richard Bros	GNL840N	Silcox
G51OUB	Davies Bros	G239FJC	Crosville	G990FVV	Mid Wales Motorways	GNT435V	Bryn Melyn
G63SNN	Davies Bros	G240FJC	Crosville	GBD777T	Lewis Y Llan	GOG554N	P & O Lloyd

Ieuan Williams' fleet of buses has been complemented recently by the purchase of two new Mercedes-Benz midibuses. Gwynedd County Council tenders specify requirements that often include aspects of the livery to denote their involvement. In 1992 a Dormobile Routemaker-bodied vehicle, K542OGA, arrived in all white livery that is still retained and is seen at Cardiff for a rugby international. Wrights supplied the 1995 addition and that arrived in an all-yellow livery.

Reg	Operator	Reg	Operator	Reg	Operator	Reg	Operator
GOG575N	P & O Lloyd	H178EJU	Mid Wales Motorways	H880EBX	Davies Bros	HPB674N	Richard Bros
GPA611V	Voel Coaches	H179EJU	Mid Wales Motorways	H881EBX	Davies Bros	HPG31N	Purple
GPA613V	Voel Coaches	H195CVU	Selwyn Hughes	H930EBX	Gwyn Williams	HPT324H	Davies Bros
GPA614V	Voel Coaches	H227GDE	Silcox	H964LEY	Jones Llanfaethlu	HRE531N	Goodsir
GPA853N	Richard Bros	H236RUX	Tanat Valley	HBX972X	Jones of Login	HRP674N	Ellis Travel
GRF697V	Clynnog & Trefor	H272LJC	Lewis Y Llan	HCC852	Purple	HSC175X	E Jones & Son
GRF712V	Alpine	H273LJC	Lewis Y Llan	HCS793N	Davies Bros	HSD78V	Tanat Valley
GSK676	Silcox	H332FEJ	Richard Bros	HDE250N	Silcox	HSD84V	Tanat Valley
GTO300V	P & O Lloyd	H399CJF	Browns of Builth	HDE611N	Silcox	HSU548	Clynnog & Trefor
GTX359N	Silver Star	H466LEY	Goodsir	HDE612N	Silcox	HSV674	Fisher
GTX361N	Silver Star	H482SWE	Nefyn Coaches	HDE617N	Silcox	HSV723	Oare's of Holywell
GUG929Y	Fisher	H521YCX	Arvonia	HDF700L	Meyers	HUD495W	Devaway
GVJ522X	James Brothers	H533MCC	Nefyn Coaches	HED203V	Devaway	HUD496W	Devaway
GWD777T	Berwyn	H544KSG	Berwyn	HEN867N	Purple	HUD498W	Devaway
GWE502V	Cerbydau Cenarth	H547EVM	Carreglefn Cs	HEU350	Williams, Cwmdu	HUD501W	Devaway
GWO1L	Williams, Cwmdu	H595EBX	Davies Bros	HEY78Y	Williams - Bala	HUI4199	Oare's of Holywell
GWY961J	Empire Goldstar	H606UWR	Silver Star	HFM962T	Voel Coaches	HUP768T	Alpine
H2WJI.	Lewis Whitland	H650REP	Gwyn Williams	HFX401V	Longs	HUX18V	Fisher
H9CCH	Jones Llanfaethlu	H694FFJ	Gwyn Williams	HHA183L	Express Motors	HUX20V	Fisher
H10WMW	Gwyn Williams	H704FDE	Richard Bros	HHG25	Alpine	HVC9V	Richard Bros
H16TBC	Thomas Bros	H712BRG	Clwydian Tours	HIL3140	Acton Coaches	HWY719N	Silcox
H20DBW	Gwyn Williams	H736EDE	Silcox	HIL5659	M & H Travel	IIL6252	P & O Lloyd
H26ARK	Summerdale	H738TWB	Chaloner's	HIL7592	Crosville	IIL8518	Williams, Cwmdu
H28MJN	Crosville	H741TWB	Nefyn Coaches	HIL7593	Crosville	IIL8519	Williams, Cwmdu
H29MJN	Crosville	H742TWB	Nefyn Coaches	HIL7896	Cross Gates Cs	IIL8520	Williams, Cwmdu
H61WNN	Davies Bros	H743EDE	Silcox	HJB460W	Alpine	IIL8521	Williams, Cwmdu
H130LPU	Crosville	H754EDE	Silcox	HJB463W	Alpine	IIL8522	Williams, Cwmdu
H14JYM	Prestatyn Cs	H759RNT	Celtic	HJP472V	Ellis Travel	IIL8744	P & O Lloyd
H154DVM	Selwyn Hughes	H825RWJ	Cross Gates Cs	HMA558T	Crosville	J37VDW	Caelloi
H158HDE	Richard Bros	H831AHS	Selwyn Hughes	HMA563T	Crosville	J38VDW	Caelloi
H160NBF	Williams, Cwmdu	H838NOC	Nefyn Coaches	HMA564T	K M P	J59NJT	K M P
H168DJU	Eagles & Crawford	H879EBX	Davies Bros	HMA571T	Crosville	J64PDE	Richard Bros

Cross Gates have operated Scania products for eleven years, their first being a former British Airways Van-Hool bodied K112. Their first new Scania arrived in March 1996 and introduced a new livery style which will extend to all front-line vehicles in due course. N10CGC, an Irizar Century-bodied K113 was photographed shortly after delivery. *David Donati*

J111SEL	Selwyn Hughes	JKO64N	Richard Bros	K367TJF	E Jones Passenger	KRN107T	Tanat Valley
J117NJT	K M P	JLJ109V	Davies Bros	K457BRE	Royal Mail	KRN111T	Tanat Valley
J133UUH	Royal Mail	JMB403T	Crosville	K498BRE	Royal Mail	KSO74P	Jones Llanfaethlu
J189BWJ	Longs	JMB404T	Clynnog & Trefor	K499RBX	Davies Bros	KSU409	Silcox
J198PEY	Silver Star	JPL105K	Alpine	K511WTT	Royal Mail	KSU477	Stratos Travel
J221HDS	Arvonia	JST905Y	Berwyn	K530RJX	Richard Bros	KSU490	Stratos Travel
J248SOC	Berwyn	JTD390P	Crosville	K5420GA	Williams Deiniolen	KTT38P	Thomas Bros
J291RNE	P & O Lloyd	JTD395P	Crosville	K647RDE	Jones of Login	KTT40P	Silcox
J387ODE	Silcox	JTH780P	Jones Llanfaethlu	K648RDE	Jones of Login	KUY442X	Ffoshelig
J544DJV	Bryn Melyn	JTH785P	Jones Llanfaethlu	K649RDE	Jones of Login	KYC984V	Celtic
J691XUX	Owen's	JTM114V	Richard Bros	K650RDE	Jones of Login	KYU88X	Berwyn
J771VFA	Royal Mail	JTU572T	Crosville	K651TDE	Silcox	L2ARV	Arvonia
J823VUJ	Royal Mail	JTU573T	Crosville	K665EEH	Royal Mail	L3VLT	Vale of Llangollen
J824VUJ	Royal Mail	JTU574T	Crosville	K698BFA	Royal Mail	L4VLT	Vale of Llangollen
J825VUJ	Royal Mail	JTU576T	Crosville	K699BFA	Royal Mail	L5VLT	Vale of Llangollen
J826VUJ	Royal Mail	JTU589T	Crosville	K703BFA	Royal Mail	L6VLT	Vale of Llangollen
J841VUJ	Royal Mail	JTU590T	Crosville	K805SCC	Nefyn Coaches	L10CAE	Caelloi
J912PEY	Bryn Melyn	JTU596T	K M P	K812EET	Stratos Travel	L35OKV	Crosville
J918ODE	Jones of Login	JTU597T	Goodsir	K856CEH	Royal Mail	L36OKV	Crosville
J986UCY	Longs	JTU600T	Crosville	KBU912P	Alpine	L37OKV	Crosville
J987GLG	Vale of Llangollen	JTV465V	Cerbydau Cenarth	KCG614L	Williams Deiniolen	L38OKV	Crosville
JAB7T	Alpine	JUH229W	Jones of Login	KCO524P	Purple	L77KMP	K M P
JAZ9864	Stafford's	JUH230W	Jones of Login	KCX945N	Mid Wales Motorways	L128VEG	Royal Mail
JBH390V	M & H Travel	JVJ511Y	Browns of Builth	KCY187P	Longs	L261VSU	D & G Coaches
JBR692T	Jones Llanfaethlu	JWG193P	Jones Llanfaethlu	KDE161L	Silcox	L458VBX	Davies Bros
JC8344	Great Orme Tours	JWU335J	Silver Star	KFM191T	P & O Lloyd	L478WBX	Davies Bros
JC9736	Voel Coaches	JWW226N	K M P	KFO181Y	Williams, Cwmdu	L485XDE	Richard Bros
JDT436N	Jones Llanfaethlu	JYG432V	Devaway	KGD54T	Jones Llanfaethlu	L495XNR	Bryn Melyn
JFK866V	Bryn Melyn	JYG435V	Devaway	KGD778T	D & G Coaches	L710LFO	Browns of Builth
JIL4404	P & O Lloyd	K4CYM	T S Lewis	KHU326P	Thomas Bros	L715WCC	Crosville
JIL5230	Gwyn Williams	K4DAF	Lewis Whitland	KJC97	Carreglefn Cs	L716WCC	Crosville
JIL5231	Gwyn Williams	K27EWC	Crosville	KJO502W	Devaway	L717WCC	Crosville
JKO62N	Richard Bros	K123DNT	Stratos Travel	KON302P	P & O Lloyd	L725JUX	Selwyn Hughes
JKO63N	Richard Bros	K182RBX	Davies Bros	KON358P	P & O Lloyd	L777KMP	K M P

Reg	Operator	Reg	Operator	Reg	Operator	Reg	Operator
L975VDE	Jones of Login	M713YJC	Crosville	N995CCC	Crosville	OKW525R	P & O Lloyd
LAL746P	Thomas Bros	M714YJC	Crosville	N996CCC	Crosville	OKY76X	Summerdale
LBU630V	Longs	M740DDE	Richard Bros	N997CCC	Crosville	OLG1V	Eagles & Crawford
LBX861P	Davies Bros	M777KMP	K M P	NAB848T	Williams, Cwmdu	OLG601V	Phillips
LBZ7534	Cerbydau Cenarth	M794MTH	Ffoshelig	NCD551M	Mid Wales Motorways	OOR320G	Lewis Whitland
LDC78P	Alpine	M798DDE	Richard Bros	NDE86R	Silcox	OOS923V	Rogers
LDE163P	Silcox	M829VCA	Clwydian Tours	NDE481Y	Richard Bros	OPL77W	Lewis Whitland
LDE164P	Silcox	M874UEJ	Mid Wales Motorways	NDW140X	Williams - Bala	OPO899S	Sel's
LDE165P	Silcox	M875UEJ	Mid Wales Motorways	NED352M	Cerbydau Cenarth	ORA13W	G H A Coaches
LDE166P	Silcox	M940CDE	Edward Bros	NEY819	Purple	OSJ622R	Silcox
LDE547P	Richard Bros	M979HDV	Royal Mail	NGL371	Midway Motors	OSJ623R	Silcox
LDE578Y	Midway Motors	M980HDV	Royal Mail	NIA8450	T S Lewis	OTC608R	Empire Goldstar
LFT89X	Davies Bros	M981HDV	Royal Mail	NIA8778	T S Lewis	OTR411S	Edward Bros
LHL245P	Silver Star	MAB181X	Tanat Valley	NIA9778	T S Lewis	OUT11W	Davies Bros
LIB6352	Acton Coaches	MAX334X	Mid Wales Motorways	NIA9896	T S Lewis	OVK144M	W E Jones & Son
LIJ6832	Pied Bull	MBX447	Davies Bros	NIW8293	Owen's	OVK907R	Owen's
LIL7438	Express Motors	MCA613P	Phillips	NJC393	Carreglefn Cs	OVL494	Express Motors
LJT941P	Empire Goldstar	MCA614P	Phillips	NJI9478	Stafford's	OWD194	Alpine
LMA609P	Empire Goldstar	MCA615P	Phillips	NJV217R	Cross Gates Cs	OWE856R	Empire Goldstar
LPJ323P	Lewis Whitland	MCA673T	Crosville	NKE304P	Richard Bros	OWO235Y	Edward Bros
LTR997R	James Brothers	MCH351W	Berwyn	NKE305P	Richard Bros	PBH539R	Browns of Builth
LUA267V	Fisher	MCH352W	Richard Bros	NKE306P	Richard Bros	PBO10Y	Prestatyn Cs
LUX520P	Selwyn Hughes	MCY333X	Owen's	NLG833T	G H A Coaches	PCA419V	Empire Goldstar
LVO801W	Richard Bros	MDL651R	Alpine	NLJ521M	Empire Goldstar	PDE570M	Silcox
LVS433P	Richard Bros	MDS691P	Express Motors	NLJ525M	Empire Goldstar	PEH654R	Clynnog & Trefor
LVS434V	Mid Wales Motorways	MEP970X	E Jones Passenger	NMA746Y	Williams - Bala	PFA50W	Crosville
M2ARV	Arvonia	MEY395	Purple	NMS588M	Fisher	PFF317S	Mid Wales Motorways
M2OVC	Voel Coaches	MFR302P	Davies Bros	NMV617W	Thomas Bros	PIB2474	Gwynfor Cs
M3OVC	Voel Coaches	MFR304P	Davies Bros	NNM440P	Gwyn Williams	PIB2734	Ellis Travel
M5JLW	Williams, Cwmdu	MFV32T	D & G Coaches	NPD127L	Alpine	PJC630S	Alpine
M7KMP	K M P	MHS19P	Silcox	NPF650W	Great Orme Tours	PJF908R	Jones of Login
M16SMC	Silcox	MHX530P	Silcox	NPK234R	Williams Deiniolen	PJI6067	Clynnog & Trefor
M17SMC	Silcox	MIB3230	T S Lewis	NPK235R	Jones Llanfaethlu	PKY416R	Williams Deiniolen
M18SMC	Silcox	MIB552	Williams, Cwmdu	NPU981M	Padarn	PMB287Y	Summerdale
M174BDE	Silcox	MIB657	Davies Bros	NPU982M	Express Motors	PMO414X	Longs
M197CDE	Richard Bros	MNM26V	Cerbydau Cenarth	NPU983M	Celtic	PNA963W	James Brothers
M252CDE	Davies Bros	MPG153P	Lewis Whitland	NRL687X	Lewis Whitland	PNB787W	Longs
M253CDE	Davies Bros	MSF679T	Owen's	NSG216M	W E Jones & Son	PNB789W	Longs
M254CDE	Davies Bros	MSV372	Clwydian Tours	NSP330R	Purple	PNW329W	Longs
M255CDE	Davies Bros	MTV503P	Clynnog & Trefor	NTH119H	Davies Bros	POI2062	P & O Lloyd
M256CDE	Davies Bros	MVC12P	Carreglefn Cs	NUD105L	Stafford's	POI6312	P & O Lloyd
M257CDE	Davies Bros	N1EDW	Silver Star	NVJ603R	Celtic	PPE658R	Jones Llanfaethlu
M258CDE	Davies Bros	N1EDW	Silver Star	NWO731	Cerbydau Cenarth	PPT910	Cross Gates Cs
M259CDE	Davies Bros	N2GHA	G H A Coaches	OAX335M	Summerdale	PRN117T	Phillips
M260VEJ	Davies Bros	N2VLT	Vale of Llangollen	OBO631X	Summerdale	PRO439W	Thomas Bros
M290AJC	Crosville	N3ALP	Alpine	OBO666M	Clwydian Tours	PRR121L	Empire Goldstar
M291AJC	Crosville	N3GHA	G H A Coaches	OBR771T	Alpine	PSV412	Arvonia
M361CDE	Silcox	N3VLT	Vale of Llangollen	OBX345R	Richard Bros	PTH408K	Davies Bros
M368CDE	Silcox	N4ALP	Alpine	OBX346R	Richard Bros	PUF586R	Alpine
M370CDE	Jones of Login	N5DMW	Williams, Cwmdu	OCA618M	Rogers	PVO624	Silcox
M378BJC	Caelloi	N7EJS	E Jones & Son	OCC993	Silver Star	PVS43R	Williams - Bala
M411BEY	Crosville	N10CGC	Cross Gates Cs	OCO108S	Crosville	PWT274W	Devaway
M412BEY	Crosville	N10HDA	Gwynfor Cs	OCR162G	W E Jones & Son	PWW713R	Devaway
M413BEY	Crosville	N50RDE	Edward Bros	OCX670X	Edward Bros	PWW715R	Devaway
M459DDE	Jones of Login	N77KMP	K M P	ODM101	Clwydian Tours	RAA172G	Richard Bros
M460DDE	Jones of Login	N255XNT	Stratos Travel	ODM412V	Crosville	RBO202	Richard Bros
M487TBF	Royal Mail	N264HBX	Davies Bros	ODM414V	Crosville	RBO284	Richard Bros
M501AJC	Crosville	N389KDE	Jones of Login	ODM415V	Crosville	RBO350	Richard Bros
M502AJC	Crosville	N390KDE	Jones of Login	ODM416V	Crosville	RCC512S	Sel's
M503AJC	Crosville	N418EJC	Caelloi	ODM500V	Pied Bull	RCJ211M	Browns of Builth
M504AJC	Crosville	N459WEY	Caelloi	OEM797S	Tanat Valley	RDC106R	Jones Llanfaethlu
M515ACC	Alpine	N523DCC	Williams Deiniolen	OEY348J	Empire Goldstar	RDC113R	Jones Llanfaethlu
M520MTT	Royal Mail	N591WND	Cross Gates Cs	OFR117P	Alpine	RDC114R	Jones Llanfaethlu
M589CDE	Jones of Login	N709AOJ	Gwyn Williams	OIB1083	Longs	RDE681S	Richard Bros
M591CDE	Richard Bros	N718DJC	Crosville	OIB5647	Tanat Valley	RDL671S	Midway Motors
M637BEY	K M P	N719DJC	Crosville	OJC496	Express Motors	RDS250W	Prestatyn Cs
M674CDE	Silcox	N776CJC	K M P	OJD54R	Ffoshelig	RGE901W	Sel's
M680DDE	Richard Bros	N777KMP	K M P	OJD68R	Silver Star	RGF295P	Summerdale
M711YJC	Crosville	N993CCC	Crosville	OJD87R	Silver Star	RGS99R	Richard Bros
M712YJC	Crosville	N994CCC	Crosville	OKW519R	P & O Lloyd	RJI4378	M & H Travel

Reg	Operator	Reg	Operator	Reg	Operator	Reg	Operator
RLG292P	Eagles & Crawford	TJI5843	Cerbydau Cenarth	VLT149	Vale of Llangollen	XDL304	Ellis Travel
RLG426V	Crosville	TJI7518	Stafford's	VLT177	Vale of Llangollen	XEW964T	Mid Wales Motorways
RLG429V	Crosville	TKM109X	Alpine	VLT250	Vale of Llangollen	XFU128V	P & O Lloyd
RMA433V	Crosville	TKM110X	Alpine	VLT280	Vale of Llangollen	XGR445V	Bryn Melyn
RMA435V	Eagles & Crawford	TMB875R	Purple	VLT288	Vale of Llangollen	XJA562L	Alpine
RMA440V	Crosville	TMB876R	Purple	VLT293	Vale of Llangollen	XNK200X	Midway Motors
RMA442V	Alpine	TMB880R	Thomas Bros	VLT483	Vale of Llangollen	XNN890Y	Richard Bros
RNY305Y	D & G Coaches	TMJ643R	Thomas Bros	VNM239S	T S Lewis	XPP299X	Acton Coaches
RPC59X	Lewis Whitland	TNR812X	Purple	VOD547K	Ellis Travel	XRJ257S	Gwyn Williams
RUA454W	Devaway	TPC244S	Gwyn Williams	VRN44Y	Sel's	XSD602T	Phillips
RUA456W	Devaway	TPE160S	Alpine	VRP60S	Voel Coaches	XSJ664T	Alpine
RUA461W	Devaway	TPJ270S	Williams, Cwmdu	VTD720T	Alpine	XSU653	Clynnog & Trefor
RVO839X	Richard Bros	TPL166S	Gwyn Williams	VTH888L	Davies Bros	XTF467L	Phillips
RVU539R	Cross Gates Cs	TPX332P	Richard Bros	VUP745R	Richard Bros	XTH333	Davies Bros
RWA860R	Empire Goldstar	TRM15S	Clynnog & Trefor	VUP850	Alpine	XUY59V	Ffoshelig
RWE861R	Empire Goldstar	TSV798	Acton Coaches	VVV63S	Voel Coaches	XWX161S	Celtic
RYX492	Cross Gates Cs	TTA650X	E Jones Passenger	VWA66Y	Summerdale	XYK747T	Ellis Travel
SCD693X	Lewis Whitland	TUJ921J	Llithfaen Motors	VWX366X	Voel Coaches	YAD739X	Williams, Cwmdu
SCH148X	Tanat Valley	TUP329R	Jones Llanfaethlu	WAX186S	Cross Gates Cs	YAX21T	G H A Coaches
SDA637S	P & O Lloyd	TXI2443	Stafford's	WBX1T	Davies Bros	YBF678S	Clynnog & Trefor
SDL967S	Midway Motors	UAM829	T Williams & Son	WBX65T	Owen's	YBF681S	Silver Star
SEJ386	T S Lewis	UCK277	Lewis Y Llan	WBX870T	Silcox	YBW602R	Williams Deiniolen
SEL219	Selwyn Hughes	UCK500	Davies Bros	WBX871T	Silcox	YBX917V	Davies Bros
SEL247H	W E Jones & Son	UDE351T	Jones of Login	WCC92V	Silver Star	YCU961T	Crosville
SEL813	Selwyn Hughes	UDM445V	Crosville	WCD523K	Berwyn	YCV155T	Richard Bros
SFF756T	James Brothers	UDM446V	Crosville	WCD524K	Silcox	YDE350	Richard Bros
SFM10V	T Williams & Son	UDM447V	Crosville	WDA679T	P & O Lloyd	YDE679	Jones of Login
SFO139S	Goodsir	UDM449V	Crosville	WDC220Y	Crosville	YDR224	Gwyn Williams
SGR778V	Berwyn	UDM451V	Crosville	WDM352R	Alpine	YFM269L	Silver Star
SGR792V	G H A Coaches	UDW137S	D & G Coaches	WDS115V	Padarn	YHP760J	Great Orme Tours
SIB7689	Crosville	UEY398T	Express Motors	WFU468V	P & O Lloyd	YJO957X	E Jones & Son
SIB8583	Crosville	UFM999V	John's Travel	WGR144V	Summerdale	YKS322W	G H A Coaches
SIB9492	Crosville	UHH173X	K D Coach Hire	WHN411G	Silcox	YMB500W	Crosville
SJI2153	Gwyn Williams	UKG423S	Davies Bros	WIB1701	G H A Coaches	YMB501W	Crosville
SJI2154	Gwyn Williams	UKG474S	Davies Bros	WJB490	Edward Bros	YMB502W	Crosville
SJI2155	Gwyn Williams	UKG475S	Davies Bros	WJF378S	Davies Bros	YMB503W	Crosville
SJI2156	Gwyn Williams	UKH170W	T Williams & Son	WJO923K	Richard Bros	YMB504W	Crosville
SJI5619	Stafford's	ULS658T	P & O Lloyd	WLG999W	James Brothers	YMB505W	Crosville
SJI5620	Stafford's	UPC63X	K D Coach Hire	WMB298R	Alpine	YMB506W	Crosville
SKF27T	Alpine	URC158X	Tanat Valley	WPJ8S	W E Jones & Son	YMB507W	Crosville
SLO514R	Silver Star	URF660S	G H A Coaches	WRF833X	M & H Travel	YMB508W	Stafford's
SMU919N	W E Jones & Son	URF677S	Alpine	WSU259	Williams, Cwmdu	YMB509W	Eagles & Crawford
SND297X	Cerbydau Cenarth	USE633R	Jones Llanfaethlu	WTH957T	K M P	YMB510W	Crosville
SNJ684R	Ellis Travel	USU192	Clynnog & Trefor	WTL949S	E Jones & Son	YMB511W	Crosville
SNN159R	Clynnog & Trefor	UTF735M	Padarn	WTS267T	Vale of Llangollen	YMB512W	Crosville
SNU852R	Silver Star	UUX357S	Fisher	WTU466W	Crosville	YMB513W	Crosville
SSO448X	Tanat Valley	UUX841S	Clwydian Tours	WTU467W	Crosville	YMB514W	Crosville
SSU632	Clynnog & Trefor	UUX845S	Voel Coaches	WTU468W	Crosville	YMB516W	Crosville
STL199R	Clynnog & Trefor	UVT49X	Crosville	WTU469W	Crosville	YMB517W	Crosville
STT413R	Ffoshelig	VAW527	Silcox	WTU475W	Crosville	YMB518W	Crosville
SVL172W	Oare's of Holywell	VCA181R	Alpine	WTU476W	Crosville	YMB519W	Crosville
SXA63K	Goodsir	VCA182R	Alpine	WTU477W	Crosville	YPB828T	Richard Bros
SYJ961X	Nefyn Coaches	VCA183R	Alpine	WTU478W	Crosville	YPL386T	Crosville
TBD278G	Express Motors	VCA459W	Crosville	WVO855S	Silver Star	YPL387T	Crosville
TBD284G	Express Motors	VCA462W	Crosville	WWB323Y	Midway Motors	YPL443T	Crosville
TBX713	Davies Bros	VCY401	Gwyn Williams	WWE222Y	Williams - Bala	YRY508T	Clwydian Tours
TCC2T	Alpine	VDV133S	Thomas Bros	WWL439T	Summerdale	YSU446	Clynnog & Trefor
TDM769V	Williams - Bala	VIA8311	Ellis Travel	WWL532T	Cerbydau Cenarth	YSU903	Williams, Cwmdu
TDT863S	Empire Goldstar	VJU255X	Fisher	WWP834V	Nefyn Coaches	YTH317	Midway Motors
TEX118R	Midway Motors	VJU259X	Summerdale	WWY905L	Jones Llanfaethlu	YTH930T	Longs
TFP12X	Great Orme Tours	VKE563S	Crosville	XBX467T	Jones of Login	YTU325S	Express Motors
TGX759M	Voel Coaches	VLT55	Vale of Llangollen	XBX650M	Davies Bros	YYB967N	Phillips
TIB4587	Ellis Travel						

ISBN 1 897990 19 7
Published by *British Bus Publishing* Ltd
The Vyne, 16 St Margarets Drive, Wellington,
Telford, Shropshire, TF1 3PH

Printed by Graphics & Print
Unit A13, Stafford Park 15
Telford, Shropshire, TF3 3BB

British Bus Publishing

HANDBOOKS

Also available!

The Fire Brigade Handbook - £9.95

The Leyland Lynx Handbook - £8.95

The 1996 FirstBus Handbook - £9.95

The 1996 Stagecoach Bus Handbook - £9.95

The Scottish Bus Handbook - £9.95

The North East Bus Handbook - £9.95

The South Wales Bus Handbook - £9.95

The Lancashire, Cumbria & Manchester Bus Handbook - £9.95

The Merseyside & Cheshire Bus Handbook - £9.95

The North and West Midlands Bus Handbook - £9.95

The Yorkshire Bus Handbook - £9.95

The Eastern Bus Handbook - £9.95

The Model Bus Handbook - Introduction - £9.95

The Toy & Model Bus Handbook - Early Diecast Models - £9.95

Coming Soon

The East Midlands Bus Handbook - £9.95

The South Midlands Bus Handbook - £9.95

Get the best!
Buy today from your transport bookshop,
or order direct from:

British Bus Publishing
The Vyne, 16 St Margaret's Drive, Wellington
Telford, Shropshire TF1 3PH
Fax and Credit Card orders: 01952 255669